MW01600682

Published by Pozner Israel Guide
First Edition, 2015
Title: Caesarea
ISBN 978-1515014423

www.israel-travel-ideas.com

CONTENT BOOK 1:

Caesarea

Caesarea – an ancient harbor, a Hippodrome, remains of a Roman city and almost fully intact ancient roman theater. In Caesarea, beauty and history meet. Ancient Caesarea, the fascinating and impressive port city, which served as the capital of Israel during the Roman period, has transformed nowadays to a large national park which is placed next to the modern developed luxurious residential neighborhood of Caesarea.

The hippodrome and the large theater in Caesarea create the impression of moving in a time tunnel to antiquity. With a little imagination you can see and sense a Roman ship docks, right now, in the ancient port to unload its wares, you can hear the horses' hooves at the hippodrome chariot race and imagine watching a spectacular performance at the grand theater. At the National Park and its surrounding, many statues and mosaics are scattered. The view of the beautiful works of art illustrates the greatness of the impressive artists during the Roman and Byzantine periods.

You will also find many cafes and restaurants in Caesarea National Park, where you can relax, drink and dine and imagine that you are among the leaders of Caesarea vacationing in their palace.

Groundwater provided enough water when the town of Caesarea was relatively small. But with the expansion of Caesarea and the rise of the standard of living of its people, there was a need of transporting large amount of water from remote springs. Caesarea water supply project came to address this need and is considered to be one of the largest engineering projects of that period. When we moved through the carved underground water systems, we could really imagine the beating of mining tools and admire the precision of the quarrying.

One of the most impressive construction projects is the arches aqueduct at the Coast of Caesarea. During a walk on top of it you can see and learn about the meticulous planning of this water pipeline. The largest water plant, erected by the Romans, is a dam built over the Crocodiles River. From this dam, water flowed into Caesarea using the low aqueduct. You can see the remains of this aqueduct near the high aqueduct at the Arches Beach.

The Romans used the water flow lines also for the operation of many flour mills and during a visit at the Crocodiles River you can see live demonstrations of the operation those old mills.

The tour of Caesarea National Park and its surroundings is certainly fascinating and unique. An experience you will want to treasure.

View of Caesarea National Park

Caesarea National Park is built of layers of different periods. Caesarea went through vicissitudes of prosperity and times of devastation. The remains of the city testify to the days when splendor and majesty had ruled and also upon periods of recession and decline.

Caesarea was inhabited first at the end of the Persian period, towards the end of the 3rd century BC, when a small seaside settlement was founded called "Stratton" (Hebrew for: Roots Tower), after the name of the king of Sidon, which had a small Phoenician anchorage and a fortress defense.

At the end of the second century BC, Zoailos, ruler of Dor (a Phoenician- Philistine- Greek-Roman port city located north of Caesarea), took over the place. Shortly afterwards, in 90 BC, Alexander Jannaeus conquered and annexed the place to the Kingdom of the Hasmoneans and Pyrgos Stratonos (Straton's Tower) became a mixed town.

In 63 BC, the land of Israel was conquered by the Romans, and in 31 BC, the city with all the coastal zone land of Israel was given to Herod, the Jewish king of the Romans. Herod called the city "Caesarea" in honor of the Emperor Augustus who gave the territory as a gift to Herod. Herod rebuilt the city for 12 years, between 22-10 BC.

The highlight of Herod's building projects was a magnificent harbor and a massive artificial breakwater. The port was used for trade with overseas countries and therefore, warehouses were built adjacent to the port, which also served as elevated foundation for the temples for Rome and Augustus Caesar.

Herod built a city with magnificent Roman architecture at the southern part of the port. The city had all that was required for a bustling city life, both commerce and entertainment. There was a hippodrome that was used for chariot horse races and gladiatorial battles, a theater which contained 4,000 seats as well as archives taxes and large warehouses that were used for the storage of grain and commodities. Herod built his palace on a reef which contained an inner private swimming pool. The city's wealthy residents built luxurious houses and the rest of the city was filled with shops, public toilets and a bathhouse for the enjoyment of all the residents. The city had running water supply system, well designed streets, cultural institutions, community buildings and more. Despite being a Jew, Herod built the city with foreign features such as a bathhouse and temples. He died in 4 BC.

The Hippodrome that served for horse races

During the Roman Byzantine period, 63-639 AD, the city became an important Christian center, and came to its prime with a population that numbered 100,000. Caesarea was the capital of "Judas" province and the seat of the Roman rulers in Israel. At that time, Caesarea served as a delivery base for the Roman army and was a major seaport where merchant ships docked in, which made the harbor teem with life.

The sea water swimming pool at the Reef Palace

Mixed population lived in the city and there were harassment and tensions between Jews and non-Jews. In the year 66, a chain of events near the synagogue of the city led to a break of bloody riots between Jews and non-Jews, and this was a cause for the outbreak of the Great Revolt of the Jews against the Romans.

Vespasian served as a Roman emperor from 69 to 79 AD and he raised the city to the rank of a colony, while depriving the rights of the original inhabitants. Before moving to the throne, Vespasian was a commander in the Roman army and commanded the

suppression of the Great Revolt of the Jews against the Romans. Vespasian was one of the greatest enemies of the Jewish people at all time.

In the 2nd century, the Jewish community in Caesarea was renewed; Rabbi Akiva and his students worked in Caesarea and in Caesarea the Bar Kochba revolt had burst, carried out by the Jews of Israel against the rule of the Roman Empire. The rebellion was put down harshly and hundreds of thousands of Jews were killed and the entire Jewish community in Israel almost came to extinction.

Caesarea was captured by the Muslims in 639 along with the entire Land of Israel, and the city was almost totally abandoned with no remains left from this period. Caesarea went into decline and was used as a small port of the ancient Arab kingdom.

Caesarea was captured again in 1101 by the Crusaders, who renewed the port and fortified the city. The construction of the Crusaders was on the foundations of the Roman city and was designed to protect the city. They established the high wall, the moat and watchtowers around the wall. Despite the strict defense planning of the city, it was eventually conquered by the Mamluks.

Who were the Crusaders? Whoever participated in a Crusade was called a crusader. In 1095, hundreds of thousands of people from several European countries went on a crusade to conquer the Land of Israel to reclaim the places sacred to them. First, they conquered Jerusalem in 1099, and the kingdom was known as the Crusader Kingdom of Jerusalem. Then there were other crusades. Crusader rule, which is actually a European rule (Franki- consolidation of a number of Germanic tribes who shared cultural characteristics), continued in all the land of Israel until the Kenny Battle of Hattin in 1187, in which the Muslims, led by Saladin, defeated the Crusaders. Then the Crusader kingdom declined and its capital transferred to Acre, until it was also conquered by the Muslims in 1291.

Caesarea was captured in 1265 by the Mamluks, with Sultan Baybars as their head. The Mamelukes feared the return of the Crusaders, and therefore, the successor of Baybars, al-Ashraf, destroyed Caesarea along with all the other coastal cities in Israel, and Caesarea was lost under the rubble. For centuries, Caesarea stood in its ruins.

Who were the Mamluks? The Mamluks (The word translation is "acquired" or "buy") were slave soldiers who first appeared in the service of the Abbasid caliphs, the dynasty that ruled much of the Muslim empire from 750-1258. During the decline of this dynasty, the use of the Mamelukes also spread among other regional Muslim dynasties. The Mamluks were even succeeded to set up their own independent kingdoms in Egypt, India and the region of Baghdad. The Mamluks influenced the history of the Muslim empire and also provided inspiration for other armies.

During the entire Ottoman period, the place was deserted. In 1882, Muslims Bosnian refugees settled in Caesarea and they built a mosque and a small agricultural village. They left the area on May 15, 1948 with the capture of the village during the War of Independence.

A short distance from ancient Caesarea, the modern town of Caesarea community was established in the early 50s of the 20th century. The settlement was established on a land belonging to the organization of PICA (Palestine Jewish Colonization Association). Baron Rothschild, who was the owner of the land, decided that the land in the area will not be granted to the State of Israel, like other lands, but will instead be managed by a fund established for that purpose in collaboration with the Government of Israel .The government of Israel agreed to the offer of the Baron and an agreement was signed between the Baron and the Minister of Finance. Baron Rothschild founded the "Caesarea Foundation" and gave to it an area of 20 kilometers square in a lease agreement for 200 years. The Baron also established the Caesarea Development Corporation and assigned to it the management and development of the area.

Website Access

Caesarea online tours: *http://www.israel-travel-ideas.com/caesarea.html*

Online tours access code: *CAES1946*

Timeline

3C BC — **_The end of the third century BC._** Beginning of the settlement at the end of the Persian period. A small settlement was established on the beach, called "Stratton."

2C BC — **_The end of the second century BC._** Zoailos, ruler of the settlement Dor, took over the place.

90 BC — **_90 BC._** Alexander Yanai occupying the place and annex it to the Kingdom of the Hasmoneans.

63 BC — In **63 BC**, the beginning of Roman-Byzantine period Herod built the city between **22-10 BC**.
In **66 AD**, bloody riots between Jews and non-Jews.
In the **2nd century**, Caesarea has a renewed Jewish settlement. Beginning of the Bar Kochba revolt in Caesarea.

639 AD — In **639** Caesarea was conquered by Muslims.

1101 AD — In **1101** Caesarea was conquered by the Crusaders. The Crusader fortified the city.

1265 AD — In **1265** Caesarea was conquered by the Mamluk, Sultan Baybars. Caesarea came to its destruction.

1517 AD — **1517-1917**, the Ottoman period. The place was completely deserted.
In **1882**, Bosnian Muslim refugees settled in Caesarea.

1948 AD — In **1948**, during the War of Independence of Israel, the Muslim village was conquered.

1. The northern area with the ancient port and the old town

The northeastern entrance to Caesarea is through the Crusader gate that was part of impressive fortifications which included a slick moat, a high wall and sophisticated system of gates that was structured by Louis IX. Herod built the first of its kind port of docks in the open sea and alongside he also built a lighthouse and breakwaters that provided ships port services as well as warehouses for goods storage. Temples were built at various times, and also a church and a mosque watching the sea. Today, the compound of the port area functions as a recreation place. At the ancient buildings, various cafes and restaurants were built, as well as art galleries displaying Israeli art. Various activities, special events and festivals also take place here.

2. The southern region - the theater, the Hippodrome and the Reef Palace

The familiar expression "bread and circuses" comes from the tradition established by Augustus Caesar, to whom the city of Caesarea was named. The Roman Theater is an impressive structure built in a semicircle, where blocks of seats were built. People came here to enjoy the performances of drama and comedy. Even today, the amphitheater is used for stage shows of first-class artists.

The Reef Palace had two residential and accommodation floor. At the palace lived people who preferred the dissolute life of Caesarea. The remains of a swimming pool carved into the sandstone in the sea are a proof of the no satiety self-indulgence of the city leaders. The original Hippodrome was built in the days of Herod and used for the celebration of the inauguration of the city, and in which athletics and music competitions, wrestling gladiators, viewing of wildlife, and of course, horses racing were held.

At the heart of the ancient Byzantine city of Caesarea is a luxurious private bath, which belonged, apparently, to the governor of the city.

Along the picturesque seaside of Caesarea, in view of the beautiful old town, a broad promenade was established that runs to the west of the ancient Byzantine city.

3. Byzantine Sculpture Garden and Birds' Mosaic

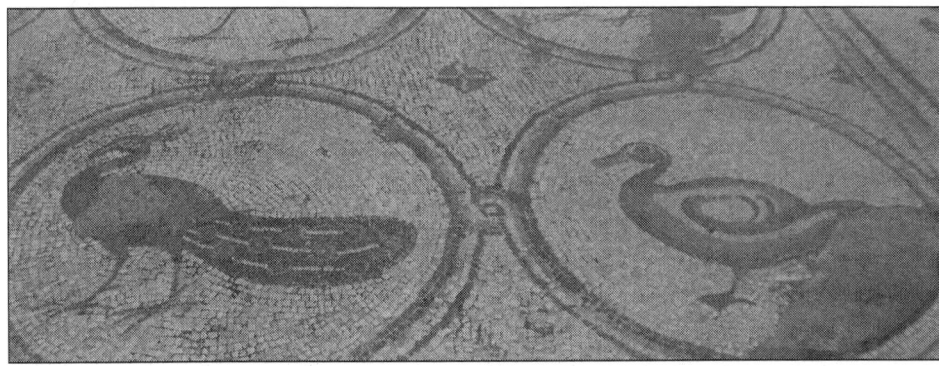

The old city of Caesarea extended in the past over a larger area than the national park of today. Outside the current national park there are other sites worth visiting.
Near the northern entrance gate is the Byzantine sculpture garden. The garden contains a paved street and two giant statues. North of the national park, to the right of the access road to the modern town of Caesarea, you can visit the Byzantine palace with the beautiful mosaic floor, known as the Bird Mosaic. This unique mosaic includes a central area with 120 round medallions; each contains a bird and a border with fruit trees and animals.
Lastly, two aqueducts are located at the Aqueduct Beach, the high and low aqueduct. These aqueducts were built using engineering skills and advanced technology which you probably would not believe that existed at such ancient times!

Another interesting site is the underwater excavations in the area of the port that sunk into the sea. The place served as a focus of interest for the construction of ports during the Roman period and for the study of shipwrecks and their loads. Old Caesarea Diving Club provides a variety of diving services for certified divers here. Divers can explore the underwater archaeological park built on the remains of Herod's port, and also the variety of Mediterranean life.

4. Caesarea water supply

During the flowering periods of Caesarea as an international port city and seat of government, there was a need for the supply of running water to the houses, to the ornamental fountains, to the baths and for water games. Caesarea was established on a high ground water layer. However, with the population growth of the city, the amount of water from the water layer was not sufficient. The shortage of water led the rulers to take control and supply water to the city from remote locations.

The water was flowed from Shuni springs, located 7 kilometers from Caesarea, using a high aqueduct. However eventually also Shuni springs did not provide all the water needs for the population of Caesarea, and therefore water was supplied also from Zvrin springs, first using an underground aqueduct and then by using an aqueduct that was connected with Shuni aqueduct. You can visit the remains of the aqueduct which are found in Beit Hanania and in the beach of Caesarea.

The great water plant of Caesarea is built at the place where the Crocodile Nature Reserve is located. Here, you can see the dam which was built during the Roman and early Byzantine period. The dam was designed for the raising of the water level and for the flowing of water over a low aqueduct to Caesarea.

5. Crocodiles River Nature Reserve

Do not worry! there are no crocodiles in Crocodiles River! The last crocodile was hunted in the river in 1912. Two rivers are flowing to the Crocodiles River nature reserve - Crocodiles River and Ada River. The two rivers converge after an ancient dam built in the days of Herod and they flows as a unity to the Mediterranean Sea.

Crocodiles River Reserve contains a large water project which was used for the supply of

water to ancient Caesarea using the Low Aqueduct. You can see here the dam, which was built during the Romans period and the early Byzantine period. The dam was designed for the raising of the water level and in front of it following the construction of the dam a large lake was formed. The Romans used the flow of water to operate several flour mills that were built in the area.

South of the Crocodiles River is the village of Jisr al-Zarqa which is populated by residents of Bedouin origin from North Africa. The meaning of the village name comes for Arabic and it says – "the bridge on the blue river." At the river and its environs there is a rich world of flora and fauna - streams turtles and catfish, various birds and also rich vegetation in the water and on the bank of the river such as reeds and the Holy Bramble.

Caesarea Association

Tourist Association Carmelim: Email: carmelim1@hcarmel.org.il. Phone number: 04-9841114. Fax number: 04-9544666. Website: www.carmelim.org.il. Sunday-Thursday 09:00-15:00.

CHAPTER 1

NORTHERN CAESAREA

Experience Caesarea, the great port city that King Herod built and which reached its peak during the Roman period.

Hello Everyone

Our trip to Caesarea National Park was without a doubt really impressive. We started on the north side of the site. Even before we entered the city, we were impressed with the wall that surrounded the site and we found that the wall was built by the Crusaders who conquered the city about 1000 years after Herod's regime. It is hard to imagine how during these ancient times, such a wall was built with the simple technological measures used by the planners and the employees. We entered through the gate that was wisely built to avoid the stampede of horses into the city. Within the city, there are many ruins, and first, we saw the warehouses used to store goods from the port. From the top of the hill, above the warehouses, we watched the city and the harbor, and a mosque was revealed to us. It turned out that there were Muslim refugees from Bosnia that immigrated to the State of Israel and the mosque was built by them. Two main things moved us deeply. The first is the harbor built by Herod and how he even imagined he could build a port in the open sea and do it with the simple technology and techniques that were developed specifically for it, and the other is the impressive complex exhibition which include the movie "time travel," that shows the city through the ages and adjacent to it is a hall with a 3D display that bring together the visitors with 12 figures from various periods of the city: we met here personally with King Herod, with Louis IX, Rothschild and others, we heard their stories and we were exposed to interesting stories from each period.

The Tour In Short

The tour starts on the north side of the city of Caesarea. This is the Crusader side. Before entering the main eastern gate of the city, you can watch the high wall which is surrounded by a moat designed to protect against attacks. From there, continue over a bridge crossing to the city gate built with two turns designed to slow down the entry of attackers. After entering, turn left and go through the restored shops street until you reach a secret exit in the wall. From the secret exit, turn right to the church compound. From this place, there is a beautiful view towards the remains of a Bosnian village from the 19th century and into the breakwater of the harbor today. The Old Port is a few meters below sea level and what you see today is a new breakwater. Go down towards the harbor and walk among the buildings, one of which show the exhibition "time travel," a 10 minute movie showing the city during different periods. Return to the artists' market (here you can do a stop for shopping or sit at one of the restaurants) and from it, pass the gate to the southern side, the Roman side.

How To Get There

Caesarea National Park is adjacent to Highway 2, near the communities of Caesarea, Sedot Yam and west of Or Akiva. Arrival is from Highway 2 through the interchange near the power plant "Orot Rabin" and from Highway 4 through Or Akiva.

Useful Information

▶ **Region:** Carmel Beach

▶ **Starting point:** Crusader entrance gate at the north of the site

▶ **Ending Point:** Entrance to the southern region

▶ **Length:** About 1 kilometer

▶ **Type:** On foot, between different sites

▶ **Interests:** History, archeology, nature and landscape, markets, culture

▶ **Opening hours:** May-August, Sunday-Thursday and Saturday 08:00-18:00. On Fridays and holiday eves, the site closes at 16:00. September-October, Sunday - Thursday and Saturday 08: 00-17: 00. On Fridays and holiday eves, the site closes at 16:00. November to April, Sunday - Thursday and Saturday 08:00-16: 00. On Fridays and holiday eves, site closes at 15:00

▶ **Phone Number:** 04-6267080

▶ **Fax Number:** 04-6262056

▶ **Best season:** All year

▶ **Duration:** About 1 hour

▶ **Difficulty:** Easy; except some steps leading to the top sites

▶ **Payment:** Yes; Payment includes entrance to Caesarea National Park and the audiovisual exposition in one card. Handouts and a map of the site will be given at the entrance. After closing hours, admission is free for restaurants in the northern region

▶ **Pets:** Not allowed

▶ **Suitable for Children:** 6 and above

▶ **Accessibility:** Only the harbor area is accessible to people in wheelchairs

▶ **Our recommendations:** Go during the sunset on the promenade

▶ **Other facilities:** education & training center, restaurants, galleries, bathing and diving beach Clarity: Very clean

▶ **Recommended equipment:** comfortable shoes, water, hat, sunscreen

▶ **Date of our tour:** November 2011

Tour Map

> **Link:** http://www.israel-travel-ideas.com/caesarea_map_1.html

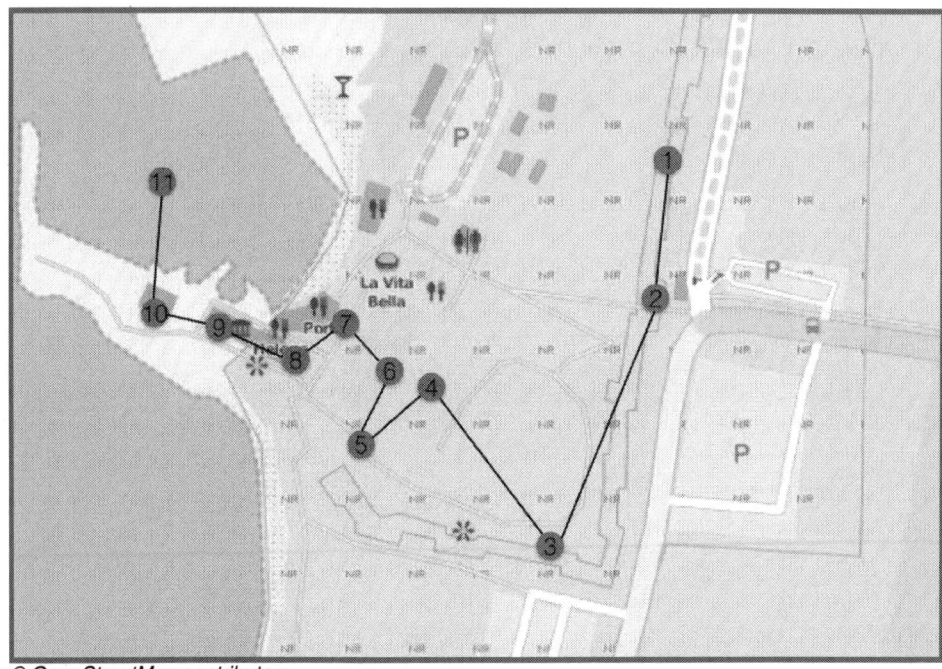

© OpenStreetMap contributors

1. The wall and the moat

Remnants from the Crusader period are the moat, sections of the wall and the luxurious gates. These structures were built by Louis IX, King of France to protect the Crusader city that existed here, and indeed, along the wall, guard towers were placed. There are 3 gates in the wall, at the north, east and south. Near the sea, on the southeastern side, a fort was established. The length of the wall was about 990 meters and 35 meters in height. On the side of the walls of the Crusader tower is a 9 meters wide moat. The moat was designed by the Crusaders to collect the

The northern moat

rainwater and thus create waterways that protect from invaders. They soon discovered that the local climate is different than the rainy climate which they were used to and the moat remained dry. Despite the meticulous defense planning, the city was conquered and destroyed by the Mamluk army in 1265.

Before entering Caesarea National Park, watch the city walls and the moat around the wall.

Go over the wooden bridge and proceed to the entrance gate of the Crusader.

The eastern moat and the wall that were designed to prevent the occupation of the city

2. Crusader entrance gate

The entrance gate, from the outside of the city

The Crusader entrance gate was part of impressive fortifications built by Louis IX. A sophisticated system of gates prevented a direct entry to the city and exposed the city invaders to attack by guards from inside the city. The entrance gate was carefully designed to protect the city from attack. This is a double gate with two turns built to stop the horses and chariots that tried to enter the city at a gallop. In addition, the paving stones of the gate are smooth so as to make it difficult for the horses to keep on running. Over the gate are windows which are wide internally and narrow externally. They allowed the guards to better protect the entrance gate together with the inability of firing through the windows from the outside. From the windows, the guards fired on the attackers or drenched them with boiling oil or stones as they approached the gate. At the top of the gate, in the center, you can see a cross-shaped stone arch.

The entrance gate, from the inside of the city

The arched structure of the entrance gate

After crossing the **entrance gate**, turn left to the reconstructed street and continue until you reach a **hiding door**.

Remains of the Muslim wall

Caesarea. Down the road is a restored shops street from the Crusader period.

At the South-east corner of the wall is a Byzantine Entrance Gate. From this gate went down a sloping tunnel with a slippery bottom that reaches to the bottom of the moat and had a secret door. Through this hidden entrance, the Crusaders were able to go out during a siege and deliver messages and other important things in and out of the walls.

On the left of the main gate are the remains of the foundations of the wall built during the Muslim period in the 9th to the 11th centuries or during the

A restored shops street

Crusader period, 12th to the 13th centuries - since the inner wall was built using items from prior periods, it is difficult to know exactly when it was built. To build the wall, architectural elements like headings, columns and bases were used, which were taken from public buildings of the Roman-Byzantine

The entrance gate which led to outside of the city walls

Turn right and walk to the **stage of the temples**.

4. Stage of the Temples

The stage of temples – a general view

The temples stage is situated above the vaults which you will visit later on the tour. The structures on the elevated area symbolize the evolution of Caesarea from one ruler to another throughout history. On the ruins of the temple built for the Emperor Augustus and the goddess of Rome, a Byzantine church was established. When the church was destroyed, a mosque was built on top, followed eventually by the construction of a Crusader church.

The Temple for Augustus was dedicated by King Herod to his fellow emperor Augustus. Augustus was the one to put an end to the civil wars during the time of the republic, expanded its boundaries and established the "Roman peace," the period that lasted from 27 BC to 180 CE, in which there was relative peace and quiet throughout all the Roman Empire. Herod supported Augustus in his early days with his struggle with Antony, and Augustus remembered his kindness and made him king over Judah. Having established his reign, Herod built three temples dedicated to Augustus - one of them in Caesarea. The other two are in Sebastia Mountains of Samaria and in a sanctuary complex to the god Pan, which is located not far from Banias River.

At the beginning of the 6th century, a church was built on the base of Herod's temple. The church has 8 ribs and marble floors and marble columns with titles. The church was built in honor of an unknown saint. According to the findings, the church was similar to the structure of the Dome of the Rock in Jerusalem. During the Arabic period, a mosque was built from which there are no findings.

The remains of the Temple for Augustus

The Temple for Augustus – A simulation

The Crusader church from the 13th century

The Crusader church – A simulation

In the 13th century, during the Crusader period, King Louis the 9th started to build a cathedral here, but the construction was not completed because one of the walls collapsed.

The Stage of the Temples is placed on an artificial hill, but which has a great view of the entire city – on the Roman and Byzantine ruins and on the remains of the Crusaders. On the eastern side of the hill, you can see the mosque and the remains of the village built by Bosnian Muslim refugees in the 19th century, and on the west is the coastline and the remains of the ancient port.

A view from the stage of the temples to the west

Go down from the stage of the temples and head toward the **port**, on your way, you will pass through the **artists' yard**.

5. The Artists' Yard

At the place where the artists' yard held court during the Roman period, the renowned artists' yard is placed today and this complex continues the tradition of art. The artists' yard was built as part of a number of shops built around a semi-circular square, south of the stage of the temples. The original artist' yard was destroyed at the end of the Crusader period.

In the early 2000s, the Caesarea Development Corporation (CDC) renewed the picturesque artists' compound and launched six new galleries and a cafe. The complex is located in-between the beautiful antiques and offers a new and diverse mix of work of art and gifts, and also works of glass, mosaic, Judaica, jewelry and natural cosmetics.

The renewed artists' yard

Continue to the lawn and watch in the direction of the **vaults** which are located beneath the stage of the temples.

6. The Warehouses and Nymphaeum

In front of the port are vaults used as the basis for the stage of the temples. The vaults were used as warehouses for storing goods for export and import. Also on the south side in the southern part of the national park are several warehouses. Such a large quantity of warehouses on both sides of the city indicates the large volume of trade that was conducted in the days of Herod the Great.

Vaults used as warehoused and above them are the temples

The Nymphaeum, a public water fountain

Artistic restoration of the Nymphaeum

North of the warehouses is the Nymphaeum, a public water fountain decorated with Roman statues, which was filling up from the aqueduct. This is a magnificent historical relic of 2000 years old that was used in ancient times, in the Roman period, for decoration, drink, and as a central place for gatherings.

A pool was discovered at the front of the building with sculptures inside niches in its wall. An aqueduct which supplied water to the city, reached the main fountain, from which residents could draw water to their homes.

Face east and **walk toward the port**, on your way you will pass a few points of interest.

7. Sarcophagi

Sarcophagus is a stone coffin, the origin of the word is in Greek, meaning "meat eater." The picture of the sarcophagus below is decorated with garlands of herbs with unfinished decoration. The fracture at the top of the sarcophagus shows that it was robbed. On the cover is a burial inscription that says that the husband Elifis gives the sarcophagus to his beloved wife, Monofilo. Another saying is that no one is immortal and such is life. The sarcophagus is 1,700 year old.

8. Bosnian Mosque

The mosque and structures built by Muslim refugees

19th century, by Bosnian Muslim refugees who were expelled from Bosnia and Herzegovina and received asylum in the Turkish Empire, which ruled the Land of Israel at the time. They established a mosque and a small agricultural village. During Israel's War of Independence in 1948, the Muslim village was occupied, its residents evacuated and the rest was ordered to leave.

Why is there even a mosque in a Crusader or Roman city? The mosque and the adjacent buildings were actually built in much later times, during the late

Continue towards the port. A sign one of the buildings will lead you to an information center and the **exposition "time travel"**.

9. "Time Travel"

The exposition "time travel," a journey to the history of Caesarea, has 3 stations:

1. "Caesarea Experience" is a 10-minute film featuring a journey to the 2,000 years of the history of Caesarea with computer simulations depicts how the city has changed hands during the different periods. The film reveals the different cultures that dominated the city from the Herodian, Roman, Byzantine, Arab, and Crusader periods to the first days of Zionism and settlement enterprise of Baron Rothschild.

2. After the film, you will meet with 12 key figures that have shaped the history of Caesarea. The exposition use advanced technologies and presents three-dimensional figures. During the exposition, you will meet King Herod, Rabbi Akiva, Paul, Saladin, Hannah Szenes and Baron Rothschild and other characters and you would be able to ask them questions and get answers! There is also a three-dimensional view of the city that illustrates the visual changes Caesarea had undergone throughout the various periods.

3. The third exposition "Tower of Time," is at the top of the fortress (which you will visit later in the tour), where you can see and internalize through computer animation how the different sites in Caesarea constructed and operated, including the theater, harbor and hippodrome.

> "Time Travel" expositions
> Hebrew: Sunday-Friday, hour on the hour; Saturday, every 15 minutes. English: Sunday-Friday, every 15 minutes; Saturday, every hour on the hour.

Continue toward the **fortress**.

10. The Fortress

The fortress structure was built in the time of Herod. The building incorporates a lighthouse and protective towers of the harbor walls. In the Crusader period, the fortress was rebuilt on the southern breakwater of the Herodian harbor, and was separated from the land through a 20 meters width channel. The channel caused the harbor to clog due to the sand washed into it. In the 13th century, when Bibbrs the Mamluk attacked Caesarea, most of the Crusader residents were saved, thanks to this channel, because they were able to cut themselves off from the city by lifting or burning the swinging bridge.

In the Ottoman era, the governor house and its cellars that were used as a jail were built over the remains of the fortress. During World War I, the fortress cellars were used as warehouses of weapons and ammunition. General Allenby blew up the fortress during the British occupation.

The fortress

The fortress at night

From the top of the fortress, you can see the port, and once you come down from the fortress, you can go along the beach and surround the cove created by the construction of the breakwater.

11. Port of Caesarea

The port of Caesarea was built by King Herod between the years 21-10 BC and it was called "Port Sebastos" in the name of Augustus Caesar. Caesarea is not originally a port city because it has no natural breakwater, and therefore, it was necessary to establish an artificial breakwater to allow docking of ships and the existence of a port in the city.

This port was one of the most important ports in Israel in ancient times. Herod wanted to build a port as farther north as possible in his kingdom where ships can dock and be the first that reach to Rome. In addition, the location of Caesarea at the edge of important continental routes such as the Wadi Milch, made it possible to export spices and salt from here.

Wadi Milch is the route that crosses Mount Carmel from west to east. The route starts in the west between Zichron Yaakov and Furoidio (an Israeli Arab town) at the trail route of Dalia River, till the opening of Jezreel Valley under the city of Yokneam. This route was one of the splitting of the historic sea route into the country. The name, Wadi Milk, is a corruption the name from the British Mandate of the Arabic name of Wadi Mlih (Milh (ملح) is the word for salt in Arabic). This name was given after the name of the trail in which convoys of traders led salt, produced on the beaches of Atlit and Dor in ancient times, to the east counties, through the Jezreel Valley and the Lower Galilee, and also to Damascus.

Port of Caesarea today

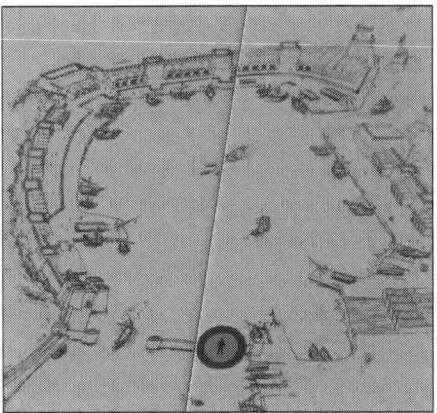
Port Sebastos – A simulation

Construction of the port was a large-scale project that required the construction of artificial islands as a base for the docks and the breakwaters. The raw materials and know-hows were brought by Roman engineers sent by Augustus to help the architects of Herod.

The breakwater was built with imported building materials, especially sea cement consisting of volcanic ash, crushed limestone and gravel, which was poured into floating wooden molds that were immersed later on. The docks were built of ashlar stones that were placed on their narrow sides and also using large blocks of sea cement. The wide main breakwater was built in a L-shape facing north. In parallel, an additional narrower breakwater was built in its outer side whose job was to reduce the energy of the wave. In the northwest section were two towers, on either side of the entrance channel to the port. The northern breakwater is relatively small and was built facing the west, perpendicular to the beach.

Caesarea, built by Herod over two thousand years ago, continued to serve nations and cultures for centuries. Over the years, the original breakwater went under and the Crusaders built a new breakwater on the foundations of the Roman breakwater that also fell and sank over time.

The current breakwater in the port of Caesarea is built on the foundations of the Crusader breakwater. During the 50s of the 20th century, members of the nearby Kibbutz Sedot Yam started the construction of a fishing boats dock at this place. According to marine excavations conducted for the first time in 1960, the breakwater from Herod time is located some short distance west of the current breakwater.

The tour in the northern region ends at this point. After visiting the antiques, you may pause for a meal at one of the restaurants in the national park and also enter the galleries to see the works of art and maybe buy a nice souvenir.

Go back to the artists' courtyard. On the right is the **entrance gate to the southern part of the city**; the southern region includes many buildings that have been preserved from the Roman period.

The entrance gate from the northern region to the southern region

CHAPTER 2

SOUTHERN CAESAREA

The southern area of Caesarea is the area where you will find the Roman ruins of Caesarea, which contains the palace, the Hippodrome and the theater that was preserved almost in its entirety. It is a place where beauty and history meet, and also a great place for an easy walking along the beach.

Hello Everyone

The tour we did in the southern region of Caesarea National Park was a very impressive experience for us. We definitely felt a mix of romance and history. We walked in the ruins of the city that extends over a large area, the buildings were covered with sand dunes, some were uncovered and restored during the excavations, there is no doubt that Herod knew what he was doing. The remains testify to the glorious past of the site. With a little imagination, we could really feel the pomp and splendor that distinguished the city, for example, in the Roman Theater where dance and drama performances were held. In our imagination, we could see the hordes of people watching the races in the Hippodrome and cheer to the winners and imagine Caesarea's rich vacationers at Herod's palace that dip in the pool that was carved in the sea. Finally, in the evening, we walked along the promenade that was built along the beach and watched the sun set slowly. Truly recommended!

The Tour In Short

After exiting the southern wall gate *(Northern Region - Chapter 1)*, you will continue south to the Hippodrome, which was used for chariot races horses. On the left are large warehouses, which used to store grain and goods brought from the port. Turn left, to the east, to the commercial area and you will pass along a mosaic of mountain goats, public toilets and the archives taxes structure. Turn right next to the Rich house and the bathhouse beside it, where you can see magnificent mosaics. Then you will go back towards the Hippodrome where you can see the archaeological section indicating the accumulation of layers of Caesarea. On the south side of the racecourse, you will go up the stairs to the Palace of Herod. This palace contained an inner luxurious private swimming pool. Continue east and through the gate, you will enter an impressive garden where you can learn about the old Roman architecture such as the column titles. Finally, you will reach the Amphitheater, which has 4000 seats, two wings, an orchestra stand, and a backstage wall that served as a backdrop and a place for stage sets.

How To Get There

Caesarea National Park is adjacent to Highway 2, near the communities of Caesarea, Sedot Yam and west of Or Akiva. Arrival is from Highway 2 through the interchange near the power plant "Orot Rabin" and from Highway 4 through Or Akiva.

➤ **Region:** Carmel Beach

➤ **Starting point:** Crusader entrance gate at the north of the site

➤ **Ending Point:** Entrance to the southern region

➤ **Length:** About 1 kilometer

➤ **Type:** On foot

➤ **Interests:** History, archeology, nature and landscape, markets, culture

➤ **Opening hours:** May-August, Sunday-Thursday and Saturday 08:00-18:00. On Fridays and holiday eves, the site closes at 16:00. September-October, Sunday - Thursday and Saturday 08: 00-17: 00. On Fridays and holiday eves, the site closes at 16:00. November to April, Sunday - Thursday and Saturday 08:00-16: 00. On Fridays and holiday eves, site closes at 15:00

➤ **Phone Number:** 04-6267080

➤ **Fax Number:** 04-6262056

➤ **Facebook:** https://www.facebook.com/caesareaNpalL

➤ **Best season:** All year.

➤ **Duration:** 1.5 to 2 hours.

➤ **Difficulty:** Easy; except some steps leading to the top sites

➤ **Payment:** Yes; Payment includes entrance to Caesarea National Park and the audiovisual exposition in one card. Handouts and a map of the site will be given at the entrance. After closing hours, admission is free for restaurants in the northern region

➤ **Pets:** Not allowed

➤ **Suitable for Children:** 6 and above

➤ **Accessibility:** The theater, the submerged reef sea palace, the archaeological findings garden, the promenade of the racecourse, andthe ancient Crusader city are all accessible to people in wheelchairs

➤ **Our recommendations:** Visit the beach promenade during sunset

➤ **Cleanliness:** Very clean

➤ **Recommended equipment:** comfortable shoes, water, hat, sunscreen

➤ **Date of our tour:** November 2011

Tour Map

Link: http://www.israel-travel-ideas.com/caesarea_map_2.html

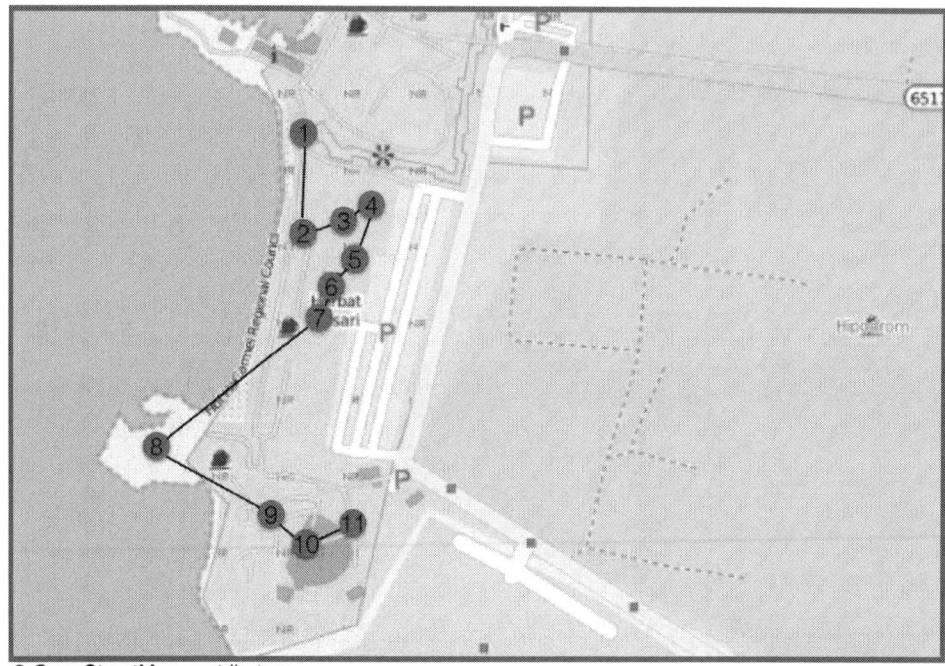

© OpenStreetMap contributors

1. Anchors Plaza

Observation from the Northern region toward the southern region

After you left the **Northern region** toward the Southern region, look to the right and in front of you, you will find the **anchors broad.**

The anchors plaza

The ancient anchors, used in ancient times, were actually rocks. In this way, based on the weight alone, the anchor is used only as a permanent anchor. A transfer of such an anchor to a different place is almost impossible and therefore, when the sailors wanted to sail, they cut the rope and the anchor remained at the bottom of the sea.

2. The Hippodrome

The Hippodrome, a view from the South

full moon nearest the longest day year, in 432 BC.

At the Hippodrome, horse and chariot racing were held for two or four horses. You can just imagine the intensity of the enthusiasm of the spectators when the carriages left the starting gate, for race of 7 laps. It is nice to note that the starting positions were arranged in an array that would provide equal opportunities for all competitors.

According to the description of Josephus Flavius in his book, 'Antiquities of the Jews': *"The whole building came to an end in the tenth year, while the date of inauguration took place in the twenty-eight of his (Herod) reign during the hundred and ninety-two Olympics. Immediately upon the inauguration of the city, great celebrations and excessive spending preparations took place, as the competitions announced in music (Musicim) and games (Gimnyakiim), and prepared a lot of great fighters and animal and horse racing..."*

The Olympics was held in four-year cycles which were actually used as the calendar of ancient Greece. This cycle is associated with the Olympic Games that were held in Greece. The Olympics period began with the opening of the Games in the Greek New Year - the first

The Hippodrome games were founded by Herod in honor of the victory of Emperor Augustus in the Battle of Actium. The games were held every four years and included athletic performances, gladiatorial battles, hunting games and instigating of animals against each other.

The length of the Hippodrome is 315 meters and 68 meters wide. The area of the Hippodrome was split along its entire length to two routes using a long and low structure with a magnificent obelisk on top of it. There are remains in the area of granite stones which were the lower part of the high columns that were designed to excite the horses during the race. The racing of horse-drawn carriages took place around the elongated structure. On the eastern side of the Hippodrome were

The starting gate of the carriages

The seats of the masses

10,000 seats for the masses in 12 rows of stairs and above them were seats for the notables of the city.

During the Roman period, in the first and second AD, the Hippodrome went through changes. At the last stage of its existence, the arena was reduced to one third of its original length, and the southern part of the building became an oval shaped amphitheater, which was used for the war of gladiators and hunting shows. During the Byzantine period, the arena was filled with debris and covered with public buildings that were built in its territory.

On the eastern side of the **Hippodrome**, you will notice the **arches**.

3. The six warehouses assembly

Vaults built as a basis for the administrative and commercial area

On the eastern side of the Hippodrome, there are 6 parallel elongated arches (vaults) facing the sea. The arches are in the form of a half horizontally cylinder. They were built from a long series of arches linked to each other in order to form the shape of a cylinder. These vaults were built as the basis of the Byzantine palace and of the administrative and commercial area. Later, the vaults were also used for storage. The large number of warehouses reflects the prosperity of the city. The warehouses were used for the international trading at the port and also for long term storage of products sold in the city markets. The warehouses were used primarily for storing of liquids, such as oil and wine, which were stored in jars, and also for grains.

Before the **Hippodrome**, face east, and walk toward the **commercial area**.

The commercial area

Like many other cities built by the Romans, the city's planning was based on an orderly grid of north-south and east-west streets, which at their center, undergo two main streets. "Cardo Maximus" on the north-south axis and "Dkomnos Maximus" on the east-west axis and beside them, the Romans built shops and public buildings.

The commercial area of the city was built over the vaults which functioned as storerooms as we just learned. At the shops street there were vaults, some of which were used as storerooms. One of the vaults was used as a tavern and others were used as corridors or as the basis for the Byzantine palace.

The Ibex Mosaic

At the area of the Old City, richly decorated buildings were discovered. In the northeast corner of the commercial area is an ibex mosaic, a mosaic floor of vine leaves and among them birds and animals with horns and a pair of mountain goats. Other decorated buildings are found in different areas of the city.

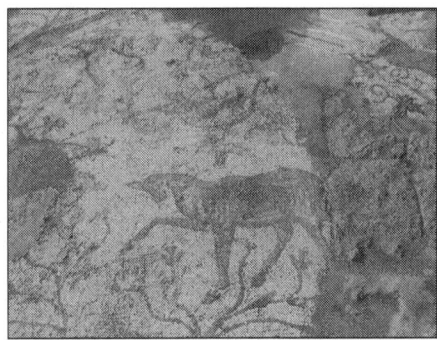

The Ibex Mosaic

The taxes building / Byzantine palace

The Byzantine palace was built for the Roman governor that was in charge of collecting taxes. The tax repository is located in the center of the commercial area, it is a rectangular hall surrounded by rooms on all sides and it was part of

The paved street

Palace of the Byzantine governor

the Government district. At the Byzantine palace, a mosaic was exposed that was created using the Opus Sectile technique - this method include the use of colored flooring slabs with different geometric shapes. The mosaic is surrounded by stone benches which were used as waiting places - a bureaucratic system is a clear sign of Roman rule; hence it was probably necessary to wait for long stretches of time. The inscription on the mosaic says: "If you comply with the tax authorities, you do not have anything to fear."

The entire structure was built on a raised floor and it is estimated that it met the need to lower the humidity in buildings where moisture sensitive documents were found.

During the Byzantine era, the palace became the residence of the Byzantine governor who coordinated the powers in law, management and taxes.

The Tavern vault

The Tavern
One of the vaults adjacent to the Byzantine palace was used as taverns.

Taverna means "cabin," a restaurant serving Greek cuisine.

Public toilet
A public toilet facility is typical of a Roman-Byzantine city. Along the southern and western walls of the toilet, marble benches were installed and below them, water flowed into the trenches. These trenches were drained to the main sewer under Decumanus Street, the east-west street.

The public toilet facility

5. The riches House

The Riches House overlooking the sea

The sunken garden palace

During the Byzantine period, a class of traders and government officials had grown in Caesarea. They made sure to build lavish palaces and villas for themselves. One of those houses is the Riches House built in the sixth century AD. This is a three levels house overlooking the sea and it includes a "sunken" garden surrounded by narrow columns and systems of rooms and halls decorated with mosaic floors, wall paintings and marble decorations.

6. The Bathhouse

The bathhouse was built during the Byzantine period and includes a number of rooms. Passage through the bath house includes three stages. Passing from the cold room to the lukewarm water room and finally to the hot water room.

The hot room had a double floor; on the lower floor were columns of a height of about 50 to 60 centimeters with stone slabs on top of them that formed the pavement of the hot room. Adjacent to the walls of the hot room, beneath the lower floor, fire was burning, the flames and the hot air created by the fire moved to the space between the lower and upper floor and between the columns. The room also had chimneys, through which the hot air could move and in this way, the walls of the room were also warmed up.

This sequence of moving from the cold room to the hot room helps opening the pores of the body and cleanses the skin. Upon visiting the building, you can see the walls and floor with the pipes that were used for the transfer of the hot air.

Guests could exercise before the entrance to the bathhouse, and after the bath, they could enjoy a beauty treatment or the services of barbers and massage experts. These services were given at the rooms around the courtyard. The bathhouse was also used as a social gathering, here the residents talked about the city affairs and political

The bathhouse

situation, here they heard the most recent gossip and spread it and they also did business here. Feel free to wander around the various rooms in the bath house, and watch the magnificent mosaics that adorned them.

The floor in the bathhouse, the top floor tiles were not assembled on purpose in order to show the passages of hot air.

Walk down the stairs toward the **Hippodrome**. During the descent, you can see the **archaeological layers cut**.

7. The Archaeological Layers Cut

The archaeological incision indicates the deposit of soil and fragments of building blocks. The analysis of the site allows understanding the processes of construction, destruction and accumulation of layers, and also restoring, through the use of those layers, the history of Caesarea.

The accumulation of layers of the history of Caesarea

Continue to the **Hippodrome**, walk to the south, and go up the stairs that are closer to the sea until you reach the **palace of Herod**.

8. The Reef Palace

The Reef Palace

staircase led to the upper floor and the upper palace.

Over the years, some internal changes were made to the palace, but the building continued to be used as a luxurious residential home during the Roman period till the end of the Byzantine period. At the end of the Byzantine period, the palace was abandoned altogether.

Upon completion of the construction of Caesarea, Herod planned the dedication of the city. For that, he built the theater and the Hippodrome and the large Reef Palace for welcoming the mass of guests which were expected to arrive. A very large portion of the palace was destroyed over the years by sea waves but you can still get an impression of its sheer size.

The private wing of the palace was built around a swimming pool of fresh water as can be concluded by the remaining plaster. The plaster would not remain if salty seawater filled the pool. Around the pool were kinds of potted plants that have been built to give a little green color to the rocky area. You can also see the bases of the rooms and the halls of the reef.

The lower wing of the palace was built around a pool that was used for swimming. At the east wing, a central fancy room was discovered with two small rooms on either side. All the rooms had heating room and bath rooms. A

Panoramic view from the palace of Herod – If you would stand in the Reef Palace and look around, you can get an impression of the size of the city, of the monumental buildings, including the theater and the Hippodrome. At the west is the sandy beach and the sea, and this combination of old buildings with the blue shades of the sea creates a unique picturesque appearance.

The lower part of the Reef Palace

Observation from the Reef Palace to the east

View of Caesarea from the Reef Palace

Continue to the east and enter through the gate to the impressive **Roman garden**.

9. The Archaeological Garden Exhibition

The Romans are known for the beautiful architecture of their building style. Leaving the theater, there is an impressive garden where you can learn a little about this architecture, the Roman columns and more.

At the display of the garden, there are a number of columns standing on a pedestal with the designed title standing at the top. The decorations varied according to the chosen style. The

The garden with a collection of columns and titles

pedestals were also used in the Roman world to place statues and other representational items. These architectural elements and others were placed in front of the temples and other magnificent structures.

Columns

Down the road you will reach the **theater**.

10. The Theater

Herod's theater was built in the form of a half circle containing 4,000 seats! At its open side is a stage and behind it is a wall that served as a backdrop. In the foreground, there is a paved plaza which was used by the orchestra, chorus and dancers. The theater was built according to strict construction criteria in order to obtain good acoustics so that all people sitting can clearly hear the voices of the actors on stage.

The theater was active in the days of Herod until the Byzantine period. Afterward, a fortress was built above it with half-round towers. The back wall of the stage belongs to the Roman period has apertures which were used for entry and exit of the actors, different stages of the stage surface, the dance orchestra with a diameter of 30 meters paved with

Caesarea Theatre – the stage is seen at the front and the seats at the back

marble, on which appeared the choirs in singing and dancing, the trench for the drainage of water around the orchestra and the central passage, entrances to the grandstand with the stone seats and the stairs.

The amphitheater has evolved as a public building with typical characteristics of the Roman culture. The name "amphitheater" was originally used for public buildings, particularly from the Roman Empire period. The amphitheater was originally used as a place of gladiators fighting competitions, human fighting with wild animals and other cruel competitions. The "Theater" was a place to publicize stories, to bring them on stage and presenting them in public.

The main difference between a theater and an amphitheater is that an amphitheater is round or oval, while a theater is semicircular.

For those of you who have not seen the movie "Caesarea Experience," which describes the story of Caesarea throughout the ages, you will have the opportunity to see it near the theater.

Just before the exist there is a display of sculptures.

11. A Display of Sculptures

Most of the sculptures at Caesarea were discovered headless. The Roman statues depicted emperors, gods or city dignitaries and rulers and they were used for the decoration of the city. Oftentimes, they were displayed in public buildings alongside Christian symbols.

A display of sculptures

The tour ends here. Step out of the gate and after a short walk on the road, you will reach the parking lot. Near the parking lot is a Byzantine sculpture garden.

  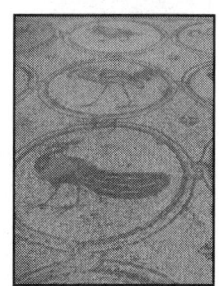

CHAPTER 3

BYZANTINE SCULPTURE GARDEN

BIRDS MOSAIC

AQUEDUCTS

Hello Everyone

During our tour in Caesarea National Park, we were very impressed by the magnificent construction enterprises that Herod built in Caesarea. From the national park, we continued to walk to other sites in the area. Right next to the entrance to a Byzantine gate is a place where there are two headless statues placed on either side of a street decorated with mosaics. From there, we continued to the birds' mosaic. At this place, there is a floor decorated with 120 birds and other animals - in the 6th century, this place was a magnificent palace. Finally, to close the long and interesting day, we drove to the Arches Beach to see the glory creation of Herod, the aqueduct that led water to Caesarea. To complete the whole issue of Caesarea, we recommend that you also go on a tour of the Water Supply to Caesarea.

The Tour In Short

During the tour in the surrounding of the ancient city of Caesarea, you will visit three sites:

1. Caesarea sculpture garden is a paved street where two headless statues were placed on either side of the streets.

2. The Birds' Mosaic is a floor mosaic located on a gravel hill which belonged to a Byzantine palace.

3. The aqueducts of Ancient Caesarea have survived for more 2,000 years; they are now standing along the Arches Beach of Caesarea Arches as a monument for the huge water plant construction enterprise.

Get out of the gate and after a short walk on the road, you will reach the parking lot. Near the parking lot is a **Byzantine Sculpture Garden**. From there, continue to the **Birds' Mosaic** and the Arches Beach where you will see the **Ancient Aqueducts**.

Tour Map

➤ **Link:** http://www.israel-travel-ideas.com/caesarea_map_3.html

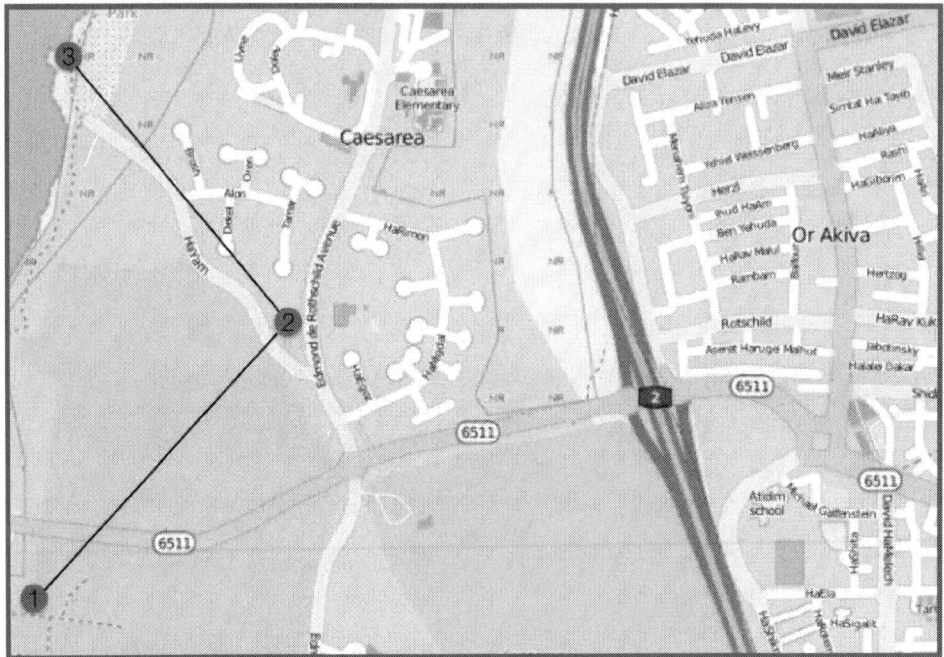

© OpenStreetMap contributors

 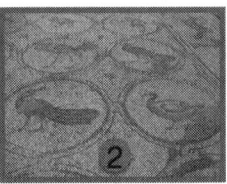 

1. Byzantine sculpture garden

Caesarea sculpture garden is a street which is part paved and part made of mosaics. On both sides of the street are two headless statues dating from the 2nd and 3rd AD which were brought from Roman halls. **Entrance to the site is free.**

The Byzantine sculpture garden is a paved street with marble slabs taken from another site. At the north of the site are remains of two columns of the original three that formed a triangular opening – three arches were placed on top of the three columns. Two statues were places near the entrance: one at the east – a red porphyry statue of Adrinos who was in Israel in the second half of the first century, the statue was seated on a gray granite chair that was not the original seat of the statue. This statue was placed by a Byzantine ruler at 2nd century AD as a decoration for the paved plaza. In front of it, on the west side, is a white marble statue consists of two parts, this statue is from the third or fourth century and depicts a god.

On the right, Hadrian's red sculpture, and in front of it, the white sculpture

North of the triangular opening, there is a mosaic floor leading to ten steps. On the floor surface just before the stairs, you will see an address, which mentions the name of the Roman procurator. During excavations made here, it turned out that the mosaic floor continues much farther to the north and to the south.

The mosaic floor

Another statue that was found in the area is of the goddess Tyche, as well as a head of a woman, both made of white marble, and can attest to the grandeur of the square. Both statues are shown in the museum at the nearby Kibbutz Sedot Yam.

Exhibitons at the Archaeological Museum at Kibbutz Sedot Yam

The definition of the term "porphyry" refers to a rock with a red-crimson texture that was pursued as a fancy decoration. Crimson was the color of royalty, and "forafir Imperial" was a rock with cagneta-brown color tone. This rock was values highly by the Romans and used in building of monuments and other major construction projects. The Romans built porphyry columns, built the crimson toga on the statues of the emperors and coated the walls of the Pantheon in Rome with porphyry tables. The "imperial porphyry" was discovered in the eastern desert of Egypt. The quarry operated between the years 29 AD in 335 AD. Working conditions in this hot and arid place was unbearable and it is speculated that the quarry employed mostly with slaves and prisoners.

Continue driving to east till you reach a square, turn left, and after a short drive, turn left again. On the right side is the **Birds' Mosaic**.

2. Birds Mosaic Garden

The mosaic floor belonged to a Byzantine palace in pastimes. The mosaic covers an area of 16 meters in length and width of 14.5 meters. It includes a central area with 120 round medallions, each with a bird and a frame in which there are fruit trees and animals such as lions, tigers, bears and more.
Entrance to the site is free, and you can walk on the mosaic itself.

The Birds' Mosaic was first discovered in 1950. The place has been initially specified as a floor of a church because of the apse facing east, but in 1985, it was concluded that this floor did not belong to a church after all but to major part of a villa.

The mosaic floor was part of a Byzantine palace, which was built in the late 6th or early 7th century and located outside of ancient Caesarea and a wealthy Christian family lived in it. The floor covered the central courtyard of the palace that covered an area of 1,500 square meters of rooms and courtyards. According to the findings on the ground, the palace had another floor which was also paved with mosaics, and parts of which collapsed when the palace was destroyed by fire, probably during the Arab conquest in 640.

Western room floor

The mosaic spans on a rectangular area, 16 meters long and 14.5 meters wide. It includes a frame in which there are fruit trees and animals such as lions, mountain goats, elephants, deer and other bulls. The frame surrounds a central area in which there are 120 round medallions, with one bird in each one, prepared in 12 rows, where in each row there are different species of birds - peacocks, storks, pelicans, herons, pheasants and more - all facing left. The order of the birds' appearance in all rows is fixed, but each row opens with the second bird appearing on the row below it, so diagonals are created, each of which has the exact same figure.

The Birds' Mosaic

Below the mosaic was a plastered cistern to which rainwater was drained and in the north-western corner of the site was located another storage pool that received its water from a well, since the palace was above the level of the aqueducts in Caesarea, and therefore it needed an independent water supply.

During excavations in 2005, a one of a kind finding was exposed, a table square board coating set with squares and triangles plates that were made using the technique of 'gold glass' - glass covered with a gold layer and above it, a layer of clear glass. Each plate is embedded with a cross, a flower or another decoration. The table was taken for preservation and it is displayed in Tel Aviv Eretz Israel Museum.

Continue on the road to the west until you reach the High Aqueduct. Then continue north, beyond the paved parking area, and on your left, you will see the **High Aqueduct**, and on the right, the **Low Aqueduct**.

3. The Aqueducts of Caesarea

*Several aqueducts were built in order to supply water to ancient Caesarea. First was built the high aqueduct by Herod, followed by Hadrian. With the growing of the city in the Byzantine period, it was necessary to supply a larger quantity of water, and therefore, a dam was built on the Crocodile River and also the low aqueduct, which was partly built and partly hewn. **Entrance to the site is free, and you can walk on the aqueducts.***

The high aqueduct was built first by Herod and completed by Hadrian in 117-135 AD. The high aqueduct transported water from the Shuni and Zavarin springs, a distance of about 20 kilometers from Caesarea. First, the

water flowed inside a tunnel and then through an aqueduct to Caesarea. The high aqueduct was built on arches in order to create a moderate slope for transporting the water. To overcome liquidity and evaporation of the water in

The High Aqueduct in the Arches Beach in Caesarea

A vault over the low aqueduct

An internal cross-section of the water channel in the High Aqueduct

the aqueduct canal, clay pipes were laid in the aqueduct. The aqueduct was built by Roman soldiers who were in the country at the time.

With the growing population in the city during the Byzantine period, it was necessary to transport a larger quantity of water. Therefore, a dam was built on the Crocodile River in order to raise the water level and in addition, a low aqueduct was built that transferred a larger amount of water than the high aqueduct. First, the water flowed into a carved tunnel of a length of 260 meters and then inside the low aqueduct, covered with a vault, all the way to Caesarea.

The basic arch consists of a number of odd trapezoid bricks, each relying on its neighbors. The upper brick closes the arch and maintains its stability

The low aqueduct near Caesarea

For our complete tour of Caesarea Water Supply, move on to chapter 4.

The view over the arch at the Arches Beach

The Arches Beach is a magical and beautiful spot, a favorite romantic place for tourists and weddings shooting, especially at sunset. It is recommended to walk on the shore winding through the coves, if you continue north along the coast of the Arches Beach, you will pass alongside a series of sandy coves. The cozy sands conceal hidden shells and Hexaplex trunculus, a snail that was once used for coloring.

CHAPTER 4

CAESAREA WATER SUPPLY

During historical periods, water was provided to the city of Caesarea by a system of aqueducts that brought water to the city. Those systems functioned since the days of Herod in the 14th century, and then destroyed during the rule of the Mamluk Sultan, Baybars. Join us on a tour of the ancient aqueducts.

Hello Everyone

Today we walked along the path of the water supply to Caesarea built over 2000 years ago, in the time of Herod. A number of locations attracted our attention. First of all, we reached facilities that were part of the ancient aqueducts that were built 2000 years ago which are still standing. We do not know what technological means was used then, but there is without a doubt something special about the accuracy of the aqueducts quarrying in Park Alona. The aqueduct path was designed without any deviations, and not only that, the planners knew how, using their primitive means, to bypass the more difficult rock layers and carve the soft stone layers and then return to the planned route. Walking inside the tunnel in the water gave us the feeling of a return to the days of Herod, back to the period when he built Caesarea and it was necessary to provide water to its 100,000 residents. To accomplish this building enterprise, Herod occupied his troops for the building of the aqueducts and the tunnels and they left behind some hewn addresses. No such thing would easily pass nowadays! Today's soldiers would probably immediately complain that it was not their job.

In the Crocodile River reserve, we saw a live operation of a dam water regulation facility. We then climbed on the aqueducts in Beit Hanania and on the arches at the arches beach at Caesarea, here too, we saw the meticulous planning, bringing the total water loss to a minimum. This was done in part by tubes that covered the aqueducts to prevent evaporation.

In summary, it was a very enjoyable trip. We highly recommend to spend a whole day for this tour and move comfortably between all sites.

The Tour In Short

You begin the tour at Alona Park – Mei Kedem (entrance with a fee) nearby Moshav Amikam, where there is a reconstructed tunnel for the transport of water from the Roman period with a length of 280 meters. Shafts that were used for entrance to the aqueduct were discovered here. At Alona Park, you will enter the aqueduct through one of those shafts and walk inside an illuminated aqueduct where the water depth is about two feet (half a meter). The tour is accompanied by a local tour guide.

After visiting the tunnel, you will continue driving to Binyamina-Zichron Yaakov road, route 652, and park your car at the orderly parking lot at the entrance to Shuni Park. On the eastern side of the road are Shuni Springs, which is the first site from which the high aqueduct water was transferred to Caesarea. It is advisable to enter Shuni site, which houses several museums, an amphitheater and archaeological excavations of the ancient settlement where the water celebrations, Miomass, were held. From here, you will continue to the nearby town of Binyamina and visit the ruins of the ancient aqueduct.

Then continue on driving and enter the town of Beit Hanania; near the entrance gate to the town is the high aqueduct that was reached from Shuni. Here you can see the ancient Roman inscription which tells the stories of the Roman legions in the area and the Tenth Roman Legion emblem. It is recommended to step on the aqueduct to see the terracotta pipes placed on the aqueduct and also get into the town, Beit Hanannia, to see the aqueduct itself. The aqueduct continues to the settlement Jisr az-Zarqa, which is located on a sandstone ridge; in this section, the aqueduct was dug again underground. You cannot walk the whole length of the aqueduct because the entrance to it is blocked.

The tour continues at the Crocodile River Nature Reserve - Chapter 5 (entrance with a fee) that combines history and nature. Here you can visit the impressive remains of another part of Caesarea water enterprise. You can see the big dam and the poll next to it that is connected to the low aqueduct. It is recommend to take your time to tour all of the Crocodile River Nature Reserve *(we recommend that you do the whole tour at the Crocodile River - Chapter 5)*.

After visiting the Crocodile River Reserve, you will continue to the last point, Caesarea Arches Beach - *if you still didn't visit here (chapter 3)*. The high and the low aqueducts, are found here just near the beautiful beach.

How To Get There

How to get to the park Alona – Mei Kedem: At Ada junction, south of Binyamina, head east to Route 654. Shortly before Givat Ada, there is a left turn towards Aviel. Continue with the road about two miles and turn right onto Route 6533. After about 3 kilometers, on the left, you'll see Park Alona where the trail begins.

Useful Information

- **Region:** Carmel Beach

- **Starting point:** Park Alona Mei Kedem

- **Ending Point:** Caesarea Arches Beach

- **Length:** 35 kilometers

- **Type:** By car between the tour sites, and walking in the sites

- **Interests:** Interests: History, history of the Yishuv, museums, religions, archeology, nature and landscape

- **Opening hours:** Park Alona Mei Kedem: Summer - Sunday-Thursday - 09:00-17:00; winter - by prior arrangement. On Saturdays and holidays 09:00-14:00 (winter 10:00-14:00). Crocodiles River Nature Reserve: Summer: Sunday-Thursday and Saturday 08:00-17:00. On Fridays and holiday eves 08:00-16:00. Winter: Sunday to Thursday, and Saturday 08:00-16:00. On Fridays and holiday eves 08:00-15:00

- **Phone Number:** 04-6267080

- **Fax Number:** 04-6262056

- **Best season:** All year

- **Duration:** 3-4 Hours

- **Difficulty:** Easy - Medium

- **Payment:** Yes, at Alona Park Mei Kedem and the Crocodile River Nature Reserve. All the other sites are free. Tourists can buy multi-tickets for various nature reserves and national parks in Israel. For more info - http://old.parks.org.il/

- **Pets:** Not allowed in Alona Park Mei Kedem and the Crocodile River Nature Reserve

- **Suitable for Children:** 5 and above.

- **Accessibility:** Accessible except to Alona Park Mei Kedem and Einot Shuni

- **Do not Miss:** A walk along the beach at the end of the trip at sunset

- **Our recommendations:** Go during the sunset on the promenade

- **Other facilities:** education & training center, restaurants, galleries, bathing and diving beach Clarity: Very clean

- **Recommended equipment:** Hat, water, walking shoes, sun screen. Alona Park Mei Kedem – shoes and clothes for walking in water

- **Date of our tour:** December 2014

During the flowering periods of Caesarea as an international port city and seat of government, the standard of living of the population of the city was high. Like other cities throughout the Roman Empire - part of the high standard of living was reflected in the supply of running water to the decorative fountains, the heat baths and for water games.

Caesarea was established on top of high ground water layer that allowed water supply from wells, but the amount of water was eventually not enough for the people and the life of hedonism in the city that included the bathhouses and the fountains.

Hence, the builders of the city and its rulers took care of additional water supply by making the water flow to the city via underground tunnels, canals and aqueducts.

How was the water led into the city? The water supply was made up of several different systems that were built at different times.

The high aqueduct

• In the days of Herod, at the beginning of the first century AD, the eastern part of the high aqueduct that brought water to Caesarea from Shuni springs, located at north of the town of Binyamina, was built. The aqueduct, which was built on arches, crossed the ridge of Jisr az-Zarqa through a tunnel.

• Shuni springs, east of Highway 652, were the closest water source to Caesarea. Shafts were found here that went down into a tunnel as well as clear remains of an aqueduct, of dams and of columns. Remains of the aqueduct were also found in the nearby Binyamina settlement.

Since Shuni springs did not satisfy all the needs of the population of Caesarea, another aqueduct was built that brought water from Zvrin springs next to Moshav Amikam. This aqueduct teamed up with Shuni aqueduct. Zvrin aqueduct was built in the time of Emperor Hadrian, in 135 AD, by the 10th Roman Legion.

The low aqueduct

• In the days of Herod, and later during the rule of the Romans in Caesarea, the water discharged from Shuni, Zvring and Alona springs, a distance of 25 kilometers from Caesarea, managed to meet the needs of the residents in Caesarea. But population growth during the Byzantine period, in the fourth century or so, required a larger water supply. Hence, an additional dam was built on top of the Crocodiles River as well as the low aqueduct, which was partly built and partly hewn. The aqueduct brought water from the Crocodiles River, located at the western slopes of the Carmel, north of Caesarea.

The aqueducts of Caesarea functioned since their foundation in the days of Herod until the Mamluk conquest in 1265, when they were destroyed by the Mamluk Sultan, Baybars.

Tour Map

Link: http://www.israel-travel-ideas.com/caesarea_map_4.html

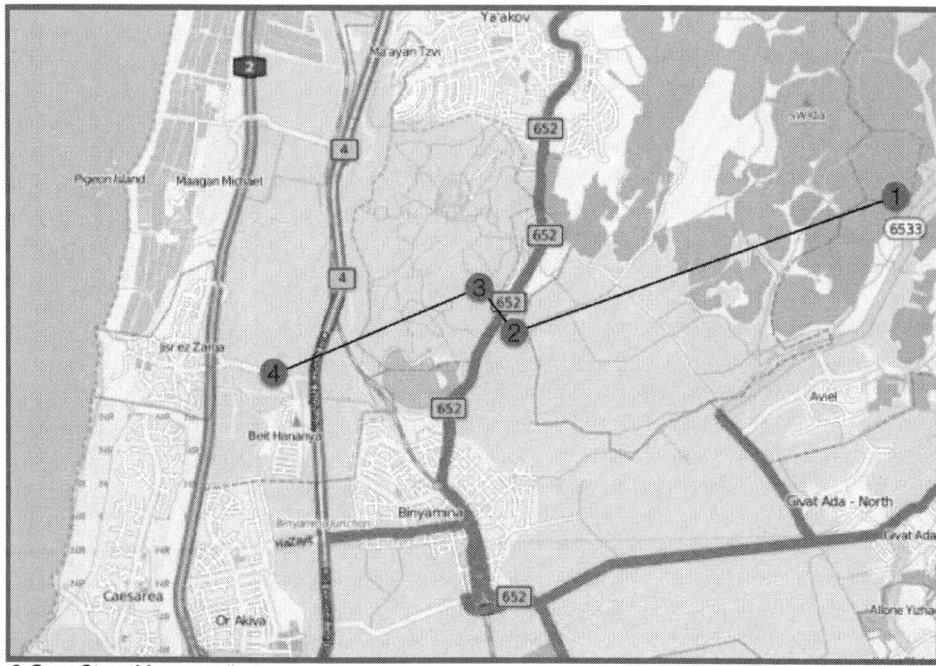

© OpenStreetMap contributors

1. Park Alona – Mei Kedem

Alona Park

The beginning of the water plant is in the area of the Crocodiles River, "Mei Kedem," near the towns, Amikam and Aviel. There are a number of springs in this area and the old aqueduct was built here. The water system passes through HaNadiv Valley and from there continues in an aqueduct near Beit Hanania and from there again, inside a tunnel, near the village of Jisr az-Zarqa, and finally reach to Caesarea through the high aqueduct.

With the increase in the population of Caesarea, which during its heyday numbered about 100,000 residents, and after Einot Shuni (which you will visit later) no longer could provide all the needs of the residents, additional water resources were identified in Einot Zvrin where another plant was built to supply water. The waterworks in park Alona Mei Kedem was built by the Roman legions that were stationed in Israel during the Bar Kochba revolt, during the reign of Emperor Adrinos.

Rock-hewn shafts were found here, which contained ordered steps that enabled going down into the hewn tunnel. The length of the hewn tunnel is 6 kilometers, and it led the water to the aqueduct of Shuni and from Shuni, another aqueduct was built, 17 kilometers in length, to Caesarea.

Alona Park is a beautiful green park so named because of the many oak (Alon in Hebrew) trees that grow there. The whole area has a rural character. Through walking in the park, you will pass among vineyards and orchards of fruit trees. Tour of the site includes watching a short film depicting the region and the work methods and tools which were used for the excavation of the tunnel. After watching the film, you will go down the stairs, accompanied by a guide, to a tour at a reconstructed tunnel. The tunnel height is suitable for walking upright.

The decline to the

HaNadiv Valley

tunnel is through one of the shafts using steps. Before beginning carving of the tunnel, shafts were quarried, those are diagonal pits with a distance of about 50 meters from each other, through which entered the quarrymen groups. It is estimated that in each group, there were between 6 and 8 quarrymen that also cleared the debris and stones. The interesting thing is to try to imagine, how, using only very simple technology that existed at the time, it was possible to connect the tunnels in such a precise way.

Water level in the tunnel between 40 to 70 centimeters

The length of the tunnel that is opened to the public is 280 meters from the 6 kilometers of total quarrying. You will see niches throughout the entire tunnel, which were used for candle lighting. The tunnel height is suitable for walking upright. Inside the tunnel, you will walk in running water, not too deep, just 40 to 70 centimeters. The nature of the water flow exhibits the precise and meticulous planning of the slope.

Due to the curves of the tunnel, you may

The quarrying height which is sufficient for walking upright

perhaps conclude that the engineering design was not perfect after all, but this is not the case, the excavation was also made by considering the type of stone. The ones that were selected do not absorb water, in order to minimize water losses along the way.

Near one of the shafts, a "strainer" was installed. The Romans wanted to take advantage of the water flowing in the Crocodiles River and diverted the river towards the tunnel, and in order to prevent stones and other large objects to penetrate into the tunnel, they built a

Niches that were used for candle lighting

The "strainer" that prevents large objects from entering to the tunnel

"strainer" as shown in the picture above.

During the walk in the tunnel, you will notice a number of memorial inscriptions, those were enacted by the quarrymen to leave a testimony to those who did the work.

Area: Carmel Beach Road 6533 between the towns of Aviel and Amikam
Arrival: By car
Track Length: About 400 meters
Type of route: On foot
Interests: History, archeology
Opening hours: Summer - every day 19:00-17:00, winter – by prior arrangement. On Saturday and holidays 09:00-14:00 (winter 10:00-14:00). It is best to keep up with the website for changes in the opening hours.
Phone number: 04-6388622
Fax Number: 04-6180028
Email: meykedem@walla.com
Best season: It is very worthwhile to visit here between April and September. The water is quite cold during the winter
Duration: About an hour and a half
Difficulty: Easy / Medium
Payment: With fee. Free up to the age of 5.
Pets: Not allowed
Suitable for Children: Designed for ages 3-4 and up
Accessibility: not available
Do not Miss: Waking inside the aqueduct
Tours: For group on prior coordination, individuals may wish to ensure visitation hours
Official website: www.meykedem.com
Cleanliness: Very clean
Recommended equipment: You should bring shoes/sandals designed for walking in water. And an extra pair of pants. You also must bring a flashlight. Notes: Entry to the aqueduct is allowed only with a guide.

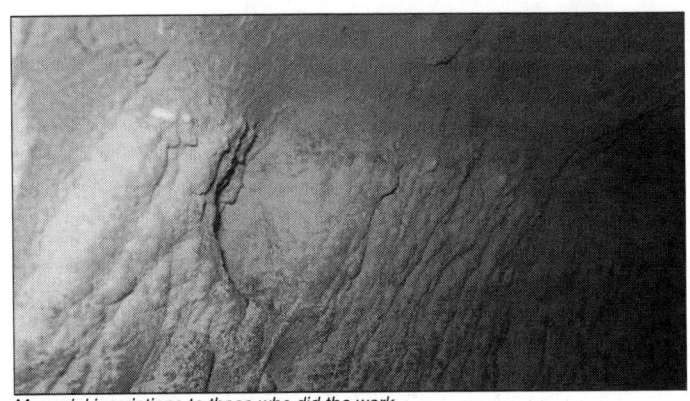

Memorial inscriptions to those who did the work

Drive back to the square on **Route 652**, turn right and drive towards Zichron Yaakov. The signs will direct you to **Shuni Park** on the left. Park your car in the parking lot and cross the street to the east. Walk a little bit north and to the right, you will notice the ancient ruins.

2. Shuni Spring (Einot Shuni)

Einot Shuni is found north of Binyamina, east of Route 652, across Shuni Park. Please note that there are no signs in the area of the spring.

During ancient times, Einot Shuni was the closest water source to Caesarea and this was indeed the first place that used to transfer water to Caesarea. At this place, shafts that went down to the tunnel were found as well as clear remains of an aqueduct, dams and columns. Remains of an aqueduct were also found in the nearby town, Binyamina.

Remains of tunnel shaft near Shuni

The water tunnel carrying water from Einot Zvrin, the springs you visited at beginning of the tour, was connected to Shuni aqueduct, which was built before.

3. Shuni Park

The name Shuni is a corruption of the name Schumi, which was the name of an ancient village that was here before the roman period. The translation of the name "Shuni" in Arabic is a grain silo. Before that, the place was called "Miomas," Arabic disruption for the Roman name, "Mioms." Shuni Park is a site from the Roman period where a Water Celebrations Theater was exposed. In the Roman period, in the third century, the theater was built in Shuni with 1000 to 1500 seats. Inter alia, water and fertility celebrations in honor of the gods Bacchus and Venus were held in Shuni. The water celebrations continued also in the Byzantine period.

During the Byzantine period, during the Samaritans rebellion (an ethnic and religious group that claimed to be a direct continuation of the Children of Israel) in 448, the theater was damaged, and then became a designated site for workshops. A large olive press that operated until the 8th century was also built at the place.

Crusaders, who ruled parts of the Land of Israel between the years 1099-1260, built a small fortress on the remains of the theater.

In the 18th century, the Ottoman authorities built here a fortress-like mansion or Khan, "Khan Shuni,"

Khan Shuni that was built during the Ottoman period

medical tool and knife surgery.

Museum Ahiam for Israeli Sculpture displaying, in different rooms, statues of wood, stone and bronze in the topic of women, Bible and music.

Etzel Museum – Etzel - *Ha-Irgun Ha-Tzvai Ha-Leum b-Eretz Yisrael,* "The National Military Organization in the Land of Israel." The museum chronicles the final chapter in the history of Shuni, which began in 1912-1913. During those years, Shuni was used as the basis for launching many operations, the most famous is the Akko prison breakout during which Etzel and Lehi people were released from their bondage.

The Settlement Museum that tells via images, a film and computerized information, the Shuni story of the settlement.

therefore, the place started to be called in Arabic, "Khan a-Shuni" in addition to its other name "Khirbet Miomass".

In 1913, Baron Rothschild purchased the land of Shuni from the Efendi Salim Khoury as part of the acquisition of extensive land area designed to create territorial contiguity between the towns, Pardes Hanna and Zichron Yaakov. The land was given to working farmers from Zichron Yaakov, who settled there, and they called the camp they set up with the name "Binyamina" in the name of the Baron.

In recent years, structures conservation work was carried out in Park Shuni that allowed the openings of a restaurant and the ancient theater for performances.

A number of museums were opened as well:

The Archaeological Museum where there is a restoration of the buildings that were in the site during the Roman period and a marble statue depicting Poseidon / Neptune, the seas and lakes god, as well as tools, ornaments, glassware, perfume bottles, collection of pipes and oil lamps,

After visiting Shuni, go back to your car and drive to Binyamina, at the second traffic circle, turn right and go under the bridge and turn right again. At 6, Havazelet St. inside a grove, you can see the **remains of an aqueduct**.

From Binyamina continue to **Moshav Beit Hanania** for a visit of the **high aqueduct**. Park near the entrance gate to the Moshav, right here is the high √, you can get on top of it to see the clay pipes. After that, enter through the gate of the Moshav, turn right and drive about 100 meters and park your car.

Aqueduct remains in Binyamina, at the south ridge of Mount Carmel

4. The Aqueduct in Moshav Beit Hanania

The remains of the high aqueduct that came from Einot Zvrin and Einot Shuni can be seen in Moshav Beit Hanania.

The aqueduct was built on arches to raise it and create a gradual incline for the transportation of water. To overcome the liquidity and the evaporation of water inside the canal of the aqueduct, clay pipes were laid inside. The aqueduct was built by Roman soldiers who were in the country at the time, this can be learnt from the address on the aqueduct near the entrance gate to the Moshav: "Emperor Trajan Hdrinos done by the Tenth Legion Frtnzis unit". Next to the address is the Roman Tenth Legion emblem.

Construction address of the Tenth Legion and next to it, the Roman Tenth Legion emblem

water on the ground. A rock that size is created over centuries.

In the third century, another aqueduct leading water to Caesarea was built, this is the lower aqueduct. For the transportation of water, a dam was built blocking the Crocodiles River which caused the eventual formation of a large lake and wetlands in the area. As a result, the aqueduct near Moshav Beit Hanania began to sink in the soft soil. Therefore, another aqueduct was built that avoided the marshes and then reconnected with the original aqueduct.

Although the water was transferred in ceramic pipes, there was still some liquidity, resulting in the formation of large blocks called Trbertin. A Trbertin is a terrestrial sedimentary rock, from the limestone family, which is formed by the precipitation of minerals and dissolving in

Terrestrial sedimentary rock, formed by the precipitation of minerals and their dissolution in water

After the bypassing, the aqueduct continues west till a limestone ridge, where the village, Jisr az-Zarqa is located today. Here another tunnel was carved, which crosses the ridge.

 You cannot visit this section.

The remains of clay pipes that were laid inside the canal of the aqueduct

The village of Jisr az-Zarqa

After the ridge, the high aqueduct continues along the beach till Caesarea.

An aqueduct was built at this place that bypassed the lake and reconnected with the original aqueduct after it. You can see the split location if you cross the road for a look at the other side of the aqueduct.

Exit from Moshav Beit Hanania, turn left and go to the **Crocodiles River Nature Reserve** *(Chapter 5)*, there is a **signage** to guide you to the reserve.

CHAPTER 5
CROCODILES RIVER

The Crocodiles River Reserve combines nature and history. The Crocodiles River is so called because of the crocodiles that lived in the waters of the river until the early 20th century.

Hello Everyone

Today we walked in the Crocodiles River nature reserve, which crocodiles were said to occupy in the past. In fact, this is how the place got its name. This is a steady river that flows all year. The blue river's water and the beauty spot in the reserve are a great place for those looking for some peace of mind. In the Roman period, water was transferred through an aqueduct to Caesarea and a large dam was built for this purpose. During our tour in the reserve, we crossed over the dam and saw the remnants of flour mills operated by water power. Down thepath, we visited the quarry gravel trail converted into a warehouse for the manufacturing of ceramic tubes built in order to dry the marshes east of the reserve. We saw a rich world of flora such as Nuphar Lutea, cane, reeds and tamarisk and also different types of fish species living in the stream, as well as turtles and the jungle cats.

The Tour In Short

There are three trails in the reserve: the **dam trail**, circular (marked red, about 1 kilometer), the **unfinished aqueduct trail**, back and forth (marked black, 300 meter), and the river trail, back and forth (marked blue, about 3 kilometers). There is no problem to combine the three trails. There are observation decks along all the trails and you should definitely stop at least at some of them and watch the view.

At the entrance, you will get pages of explanation as well as a map of the reserve. After watching a short video, you will start your tour at the reserve. The tour route will start at the **dam trail**; from the first observation deck you can watch the dam and the lake and soak up the overall look of the reserve. From there you continue to the eucalyptus grove where various bird species are nesting. From here, you can go along the route of the unfinished aqueduct hewn into the rock and walk in it, as the water depth in the aqueduct is just 45 centimeters. After about 70 meters, you will reconnect to the dam trail. You will then reach the second observation deck from which you can watch the dam. Before you get on the dam, you can watch the quarry, the clay pipes factory and the low aqueduct, which looks like two parallel walls. The trail will also pass by Byzantine flour mills and if you arrive on a Saturday, you'll see them in action when one of the nature reserve ranger will operate the mill by opening the doors responsible for regulating the passage of water. From there, you will pass along the dam and reach a restored Ottoman flour mill, and then, to a viewpoint of the Crocodile River. You then continue on the trail through a tamarisk trees thicket. At the point where the trails are splitting, you can go back to the parking lot through the low aqueduct, which is the continuation of the unfinished aqueduct, or choose to continue on the river trail till the mouth of the river. Here are the remains of the Turkish arches bridge that was built in 1898 for the visit in Israel of German Emperor Wilhelm II. To reach the parking lot, go back through the river trail and about half way turn right to the **aqueduct trail**, the black trail, which will lead you to the parking lot.

How To Get There

Drive on road 4 and turn toward Moshav Beit Hanania, there is a signage for Crocodiles River nature reserve there. Continue straight west till the right turn. After you turn, continue with this road up to a dirt road where you will turn right again into the reserve itself.

Useful Information

➤ **Region:** Carmel Beach

➤ **Starting point:** Observation deck, eucalyptus grove and dam

➤ **Ending Point:** Depends on the chosen trail

➤ **Length:** Dam trail, circular, red, about 1 kilometer. Aqueduct trail, back and forth, **black**, about 300 meters. River trail, back and forth, blue, about 3 kilometers

➤ **Duration:** 1 hour for the dam trail. About three hours for the aqueduct and stream trails

➤ **Type:** On foot

➤ **Interests:** Nature reserve, history, archeology, nature and landscape, water

➤ **Opening hours:** Entrance to the reserve closes an hour before the times listed. Daylight Saving Time: Sunday to Thursday and Saturday 8:00-17:00. On Fridays and holiday eves 8:00-16:00. Winter saving time: Sunday to Thursday and Saturday 8:00-16:00. On Fridays and holiday eves 8:00-15:00

➤ **Phone Number:** 04-6265151

➤ **Fax Number:** 04-6265152

➤ **Best season:** Fall, winter and spring

➤ **Duration:** Full day

➤ **Difficulty:** Easy - Medium

➤ **Payment:** Yes; tourists can buy multiple entrance tickets

➤ **Pets:** Not allowed.

➤ **Suitable for Children:** Suitable for families with children

➤ **Accessibility:** From the entrance until the dam only. Development of an on-site visit for the disabled is not complete yet

➤ **Our recommendations:** Watch the video on the reserve, go below the surface at the area of the dry aqueduct, and walk on the floating path

➤ **Do not Miss:** On Saturdays, there are activities on the dam and the restored paddle wheel at 10:00, 12:00, 14:00 with no extra charge

➤ **Other facilities:** education & training center, restaurants, galleries, bathing and diving beach
Clarity: Very clean

➤ **Capacity:** Average

➤ **Cleanliness:** Very clean

➤ **Recommended equipment:** Comfortable walking shoes, water, hat, and sunscreen

➤ **Notes:** At the low aqueduct trail, you can walk in the water; beyond that, entrance to the water is prohibited in any other point along the trails.

➤ **Date of our tour:** October 2014

Tourism Association

Israel Nature and Parks Authority. Phone number: *3639. Information service of the NPA phone: 1-800-546-666

There are two streams flowing to Crocodiles River nature reserve; the southern stream is named Crocodiles stream and the northern one is called Eda stream. The two rivers converge after the dam in the nature reserve and flow as a single stream to the Mediterranean Sea.

During the winter, water floods flow in the Crocodiles River and its tributaries, from Ramot Menashe (the area between Wadi Ara and Wadi Milak), and from the north HaNadiv Valley. The main water source is from the Crocodile springs located east of the nature reserve, at Kabara valley. From the Crocodile springs, there is a steady and strong flow at the stream. In the past, there were about 3,000 springs in the area of the valley that flowed to the Crocodiles River.

The river got its name because of the crocodiles that lived in its waters in the past. It is not known how the crocodiles came here, but the last one was hunted in 1912. A city from the Persian period, from the fifth and fourth centuries BC, whose name was Crocodilopolis - City of Crocodile - is proof of the presence of crocodiles in the past. The researcher, Henry Tristram, describes in his book, "Journey in Israel" (1863-1864), *"Today, we heard some rumors about the finding of a crocodile in Wadi Zarqa, this is the 'blue river' in the Sharon Plain, a little south of Mount Carmel. This river swamps are still infested with a few monsters of this kind of reptiles called crocodile by children. It is clear that this river was called by the ancients 'crocodile river' as a nickname given to it because of the existence of the creature in its swamps."*

General view of the flora in the nature reserve

Ada Stream flows from Givat Ada, about 10 kilometers east of Caesarea, and is one of the streams that are stored in Menashe. The river was named after Ada Adelaide, wife of Baron Edmond James de Rothschild.

A rich variety of aquatic plants can be found In the Crocodiles River nature reserve. Among the species, you can find aquatic plants such as: Nuphar Lutea, Potamogeton species, Holy Berry, Oleander, cane, reeds, and Vitex. Unique species of invertebrates swim in the stream as well as rare crabs, fish - Amnon Nile and catfish, swamps and soft turtles.

Squills blossom in the autumn and anemones, primroses and Saffron flowers blossom in the spring.

Tour Map

Link: http://www.israel-travel-ideas.com/caesarea_map_5.html

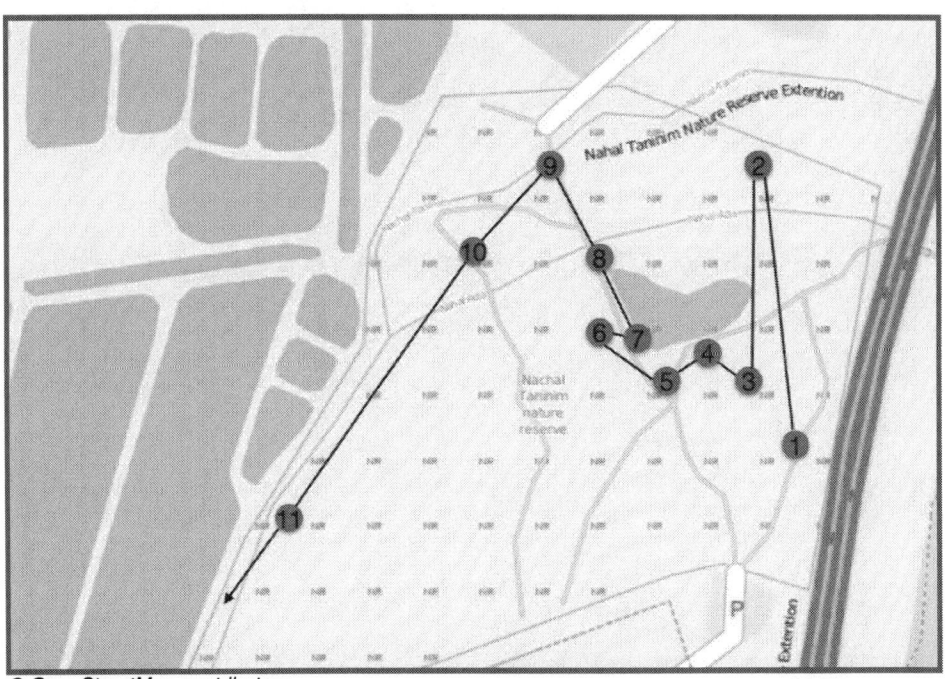

© OpenStreetMap contributors

1. The lake and eucalyptus grove observation

Park your car in the parking lot, go to the reserve entrance and after you make a payment, get some explanatory pages (You can and it is recommended to buy a multi ticket that give access to large number of reserves), watch a short video, and then you can start the tour. Go to the observation shed from where you can view the dam and the eucalyptus grove.

Continue to the **eucalyptus grove**.

2. The eucalyptus grove

Until the 20s of the 20th century, Kabara swamps in the Carmel coastal plain stretched around the Crocodiles River. These wetlands were the second largest in Israel, next only to the Hula swamp.

At the end of the first century BC, the Byzantines built the dam, which you will visit later. Consequently, a big body of water was created, the high water level allowed to pump water to Caesarea by use of the gravitation force. The lake has survived for 1,000 years, but its condition deteriorated due to the accumulation of silt and improper maintenance and it became a marshy area. The marshes were a source of the Anopheles mosquito and the focus of malaria, which caused suffering and harm to the residents of the region. In the early 20th century, doctors in Israel realized that there is a connection between the swamp and the outbreak of the disease, although most of them were not clear about what exactly is the role of the Anopheles mosquito in the transmission of the disease. They considered it necessary to drain the swamps and for that purpose, they brought to Israel thousands of seedlings of eucalyptus trees that were planted in the swamp.

The eucalyptus trees were planted in the belief that they will help to dry the Kabara swamps, which were encountered by the first settlers in the early 20th century. But in spite of many drainage operations over the years, the marshes only disappeared completely in the late 70s of the 20th century, after the establishment of a plant for collecting the excess water flooding to the area each winter in favor of their insertion into the ground water. Nowadays, there are five types of egrets birds that reside permanently over the shady eucalyptus trees. One of them is the Cattle Egret.

The Cattle Egret feeds mostly from small animals, especially insects, amphibians, small fish and small reptiles. The Cattle Egret is a sociable bird nesting in nesting colonies over trees and it also join herds of cattle, flocks of sheep or tractor plowing that expose small animals from which it feeds. 8. Cattle Egret

The Eucalyptus Grove

Now, you have two options to continue the tour. You can continue to the red route going to the dam lookout. This is point 4, or you can go down and follow the **black marking to the aqueduct route**, after walking for about 70 meters and from here, you will eventually also get to the dam lookout.

The unfinished aqueduct

Restoration of the lower aqueduct covering

In the days of Herod, and later during the Romans rule in Caesarea, the water discharged from Shuni Springs and Zvrin Springs was enough for the residents of Caesarea. With the city's expansion and population growth in the Byzantine period, it was necessary to supply more water to the population. About 5 kilometers northeast of Caesarea, there is a rich water source at the spring water at the western foothills of Mount Carmel.

First, an aqueduct was built that its construction was never completed due to error in engineering. The spring water level is 2-3 meters lower than the lowest level to which it is possible to bring water in Caesarea. You can walk inside the aqueduct since the water depth is just 45 centimeters.

To solve the problem of water level and raise the level of the of the springs to a sufficient height, the Byzantines built a large dam made of ashlar stones dam, 200 meters long, for the Crocodile River and Eda Stream that raised the water level in the enough to transport water to Caesarea. From the lake, created by the dam, the low aqueduct was to Caesarea was built. The sweet spot for building the dam was the point where the river crosses the gravel ridge.

First, the water flowed from the dam using a rock-cut ditch, 260 meters long, and then in the low aqueduct, covered with a vault, to Caocarea.

If you chose the aqueduct route, go up the **first staircase** where you will meet the **dam route** until you reach the **dam lookout**.

4. The Dam Lookout

The length of the dam is nearly 200 meters, its width ranges from 4 to 10 meters. The dam blocks the passage of water from the Crocodiles River and Eda River. To prevent the water from flooding the entire plane, another dam was built at a length of 1,300 meters, from the slopes of the Carmel to the gravel ridge, which is parallel to the Mediterranean Sea. In doing so, a large lake was created that later became the Kabara marshes, which you can read about later in the tour.

To regulate the flow of water from the lake to the aqueduct, openings were built in the dam, which could be opened and closed by thick wooden beams strung in stone rails. The length of the aqueduct, known as the "low aqueduct," comes to five kilometers. Because of the high water level, it was not really necessary to build the aqueduct in a slope because it constitutes a sort of extension of the artificial lake. Excess water, which weren't flowed into Caesarea, flowed into an extensive system of canals leading eventually to the flour mills.

Before going up the dam, continue to the **observation deck of the quarry** and to the **factory of the clay pipes**.

5. The quarry and factory of the clay pipes

From the observation deck, you can see the Roman stone quarry. The quarry was intended for quarrying stones for the construction of the dam and the aqueduct.

The construction of the dam and blocking of the drainage of the rivers by sandstone ridges and the coastal dunes resulted in the formation of marshes covering an area of 6 square kilometers. The

very harsh living conditions and suffered from malaria. The workers were concentrated and stayed there in 1924, on the ridge nearby the nature reserve, where the village of Jisr al-Zarqa located today.

The first attempt of drying was unsuccessful and the drainage engineer suggested that in addition to deepening the Crocodiles River, pipes should be placed through the ground that will lead the water to the sea. For the purpose of this operation, a total length of 50 kilometers of ceramic pipes was necessary. A furnace was built in the quarry for the construction of clay pipes, but unfortunately, the local clay was not suitable, and instead, pipes were eventually brought from France. Water of 3000 springs flowed through the pipes and was transferred to canals.

marshes were a source of the Anopheles mosquito and the focus of malaria. The swamp land was acquired by PICA (Palestine Jewish Colonization Association) via Baron Rothschild in 1922, and the Association has invested a quarter of a million pounds in the draining of the swamp.

Bedouins from the tribe Arab al-Ghawarina were hired for the drainage job by PICA and they worked there at

Go down the trail toward the **flour mills**, through the **quarrying** on the west side of the dam.

6. Byzantine Flour Millls

The seven Byzantine flour mills were built along the ancient south bank of the Crocodiles River, west of the dam. The flour mills were operated from the Byzantine period at 4th century and until the Ottoman period in the early 20th century. The uniqueness of these flour mills lies in the fact that they were operated by a wheel with vertical wings, a

technique that was not discovered anywhere else in Israel. The flour mills ceased to operate when the marshes dried up and the water flow was stopped.

Continue on the trail and go up on the **dam**, from there, go back a little to the south and stand above the **water regulating facility**.

7. Water Regulating Facility

At the water regulating facility, the doors go up and down. You've already watched on those doors from the dam lookout. These doors regulate the amount of water flowing to the low aqueduct and to the flour mills.

On Saturdays, sessions are held on the site of operating the old dam and the restored mill paddle wheel at 10:00, 12:00, and 14:00 at no extra charge.

Continue north along the dam, cross **Eda stream** and then, the **Crocodiles River**. Walk slowly and watch the stream and plants growing alongside the rivers. On the right side, you will see another **flour mill**; continue on the trail going down to the mill.

8. The Dam above *the Crocodile River*

Along the entire length of the dam

9. An Ottoman Flour Mill

the use of stone as the main ingredient of the permanent mill structure. The flow of water passes through long tunnels, which led the water into the building. Inside the building itself, water passes through a surfing rock at a height of 2 meters or more, wide at the top and narrow at the bottom. In this way, the pressure of the water striking the wooden wheel is increased. As a result of these upgrades, it was possible to use larger millstone to increase the output of the flour milling.

The wheel operated by water at the Ottoman flour mill is horizontal, similar to most of the mills that were built in Israel along the years. This type of flour mill is called "Surf Mill." It is characterized by

Continue to the red route until you reach the **observation of the Crocodiles River**. Along the route, you will see a rich variety of aquatic plants.

Oleander reaches a height of about 1.8 to 3 meters and 3 meters wide. Oleander blooms in summer, from May to August, as many other banks-river plants, which do not suffer from lack of water during the hot season. The flowers bloom in various colors - white, pink, red or purple, are 4-7 centimeters in length, and are open during the day and night.

Beware - all parts of the plant exude a very toxic, milky resin when wounded.

Common Reed grows straight and tall, among the highest in the grains family in Israel. It grows on the riverbanks and creates very dense columns, some on the riverbank and some in the shallow water. The height of the Common Reed is 3-5 meters and sometimes even more. The reeds are used for basket weaving; braiding mats, construction of fences, shelters, and even for the preparation of a flute to sweeten our time.

Narrow Leaf Cattail is a plant that grows straight and tall at the edge of water. The Cattail has no stems and its leaves come out straight from the ground, from the Cattail root; they are straight and very long, up to 2 meters. The leaf of the Cattail slightly curves around itself, which adds to its stability.

The stem of the Cattail grows in the summer, from June to October. The appearance of the inflorescence is withdrawn and dense, like a brush to clean bottles. The leaves are used for weaving of mats and baskets and the rhizome is edible.

Continue down the path and cross the Crocodiles River on the small bridge and another small bridge that crosses the Eda River. You will reach a crossroad, the left lane is a continuation of the Dam trail that reaches the parking lot, and on the right is the Stream trail that reaches all the way to the sea.

Crocodiles River - the Cattail, Reed and Tamarisk growing on the riverbank

On the right, the Stream trail, on the left, the Dam trail all the way back to the parking lot

If you choose to return to the parking lot, you will pass through thickets of Tamarisk trees, the trail passes through two corners where benches were placed under a fig tree and the other under a palm tree. The red trail to the parking lot passes through the unfinished aqueduct, at the black trail, which you saw already at the beginning of the tour.

Tamarisk is an evergreen that blooms all year, especially during March and June. It has tiny flowers; pink-white colored and densely laid out. The Tamarisk can utilize brackish water, and to get rid of excess salt and pests, it is able to secrete salt from special gland in its leaves. Some species of Tamarisk inhabit aphids that secrete a sweet substance, which is affiliated with the Manna - identified with what our ancestors ate in the wilderness during the Exodus.

If you choose to continue on the Stream trail, the blue trail, toward the sea, you will pass along the Crocodile River where alongside it, grows the Tamarisk, which is brackish-water resistant, the holy berry, reeds, and cattails. During the summer, the yellow water lily blooms in the water. The length of this trail is about 1.5 kilometers.

A quiet corner in the shadow of the palm trees

Holy Bramble grows on the riverbanks, in the springs and marsh areas. This bush reaches a height of up to 2 meters, its branches long and tangled, covered with thorns and sharp thorns. The leaves consist of three, five or seven leaflets and they are equipped with hook-shaped spines bumps, which help them cling to branches and neighboring objects. The Holy Bramble blooms in April-September, first its fruits are green, and then they become red and blacken when ripe. The fruits have a tart-sweet taste and are edible. In Israel, syrup and raspberry jam are prepared from the fruit; even honey can be produced from them.

In Jewish and Christian tradition, the Holy Bramble is attributed to the burning bush, hence its name "holy," The monastery in St Catherine's in Sinai is called the Burning Bush Monastery, and the Holy Bramble is cultivated in its garden as a bush.

Yellow water lily is a perennial water plant that grows in freshwater ponds. The pond lily has heart-shaped, non-sharpened leaves that are floating on the water or soaring above them and they can be seen throughout the year. The water lily blooms in late spring and remains flowering all summer. Because it is a water plant, it is in no danger of dehydration during the warm season.

which is included in the area of the national park, Jisr al-Zarqa beach. At this site, a city was built during the Persian period about 2,500 years ago and the meaning of city was "City of Crocodiles," which apparently proves there were crocodiles in the area already at that period. Tel Crocodilopolis existed until the Byzantine period and is believed to be destroyed by the Arabs in the seventh century. South of the mound is a "fishing village" of the residents of Jisr al-Zarqa, destined to become a tourist attraction in the future.

Near the mouth of the river is an Ottoman bridge, built in 1898 in honor of the visit of Emperor Wilhelm II of Germany.

At the mouth of the river is an ancient mound - Tel Crocodiles (Crocodilopolis),

The gravel ridge alongside the Mediterranean Sea

The gulf and the "fishing village" of Jisr al-Zarqa

Here you finish the tour that includes the three routes; to reach the parking lot, you have to go back to along the blue trail, and approximately halfway, you need to turn right, as indicated in the field, to the **unfinished aqueduct trail,** the **black trail,** which will lead you back to the parking lot.

If you have not yet visited the aqueducts, you can either,

1. Continue from the fishing village of Jisr al-Zarqa by walking along the coast, a distance of about 1 hour, all the way to the aqueducts. Note that one of the members of the group will have to arrive by car to the aqueducts or you would have to walk all the way back.

2. Drive back on Route 4 south to Or Akiva. At the second light, turn right and follow the signs to Route 2. Go under the bridge towards Caesarea and then go straight to the square where you will turn right. The next turn left will take you through the Aqueduct Street to the beach parking.

Notes

Notes

Notes

Notes

Notes

General Map

Link: http://www.israel-travel-ideas.com/caesarea.html

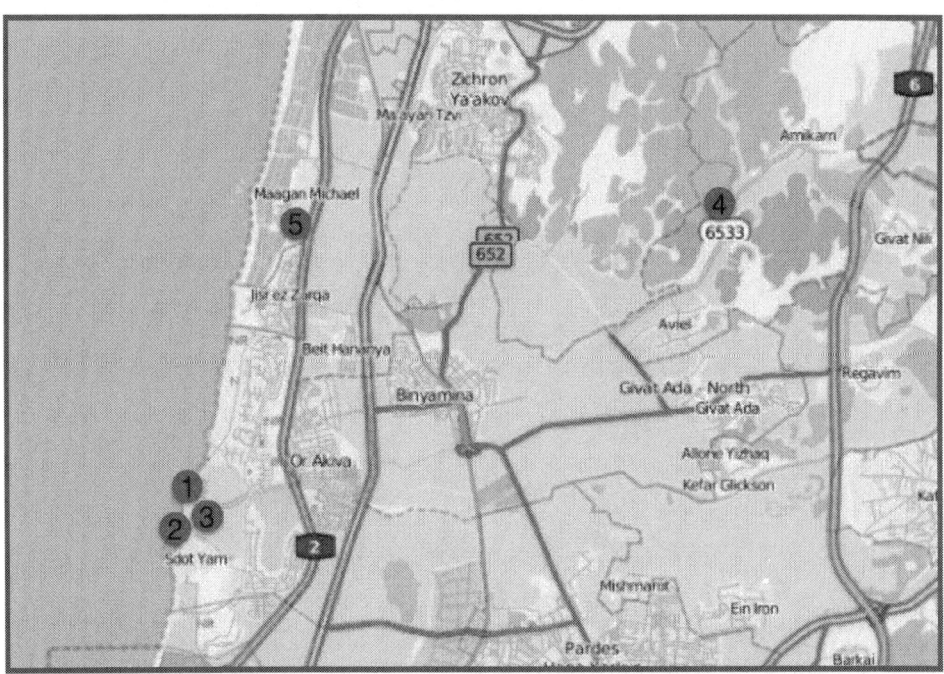

© OpenStreetMap contributors

Northern Casearea

Southern Casearea

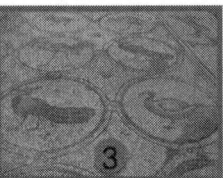
Birds Mosaic

Caesarea Water Supply

Crocodiles River

Made in the USA
Columbia, SC
29 April 2025

57316804R00052